# ST. PROSPER OF AQUITAINE

# THE CALL
# OF ALL NATIONS

---

*DE VOCATIONE OMNIUM GENTIUM*

# Ancient Christian Writers

## THE WORKS OF THE FATHERS IN TRANSLATION

EDITED BY

JOHANNES QUASTEN, S. T. D.
*Professor of Ancient Church History*
*and Christian Archaeology*

JOSEPH C. PLUMPE, Ph. D.
*Professor of Patristic Greek*
*and Ecclesiastical Latin*

The Catholic University of America
Washington, D. C.

No. 14

# ST. PROSPER
# OF AQUITAINE

# THE CALL
# OF ALL NATIONS

TRANSLATED AND ANNOTATED

BY

P. DE LETTER, S. J., Ph. D., S. T. D.

*Professor of Dogmatic Theology*
*St. Mary's College, Kurseong, India*

**NEWMAN PRESS**

New York, N.Y./Ramsey, N.J.

*De Licentia Superioris Ordinis*
  *Nihil Obstat*
          J. Quasten
                *Censor Deputatus*

*Imprimatur:*

          Patricius A. O'Boyle, D.D.
                *Archiepiscopus Washingtonensis*
                    *die 8 Martii 1951*


                    COPYRIGHT 1952
                         BY
              REV. JOHANNES QUASTEN
                        AND
                REV. JOSEPH C. PLUMPE


Library of Congress
Catalog Card Number: 78-62463

ISBN: 0-8091-0253-6

PUBLISHED BY PAULIST PRESS
*Editorial Office:* 1865 Broadway, New York, N.Y. 10023
*Business Office:* 545 Island Road, Ramsey, N.J. 07446

PRINTED AND BOUND IN THE UNITED STATES OF AMERICA

# CONTENTS

# ST. PROSPER OF AQUITAINE

# THE CALL
# OF ALL NATIONS

# INTRODUCTION

The *De vocatione omnium gentium* [1] is the first treatise in ancient Christian literature on the problem of the salvation of infidels. It is a controversial work written against the Semi-Pelagians about the year 450, probably at Rome. Its author there is reason to believe was St. Prosper of Aquitaine. This historical setting indicates at once what we should and what we should not expect about its contents.

The Sixteenth Council of Carthage in 418 had sealed with a solemn declaration St. Augustine's successful defence of the Catholic doctrine on grace against Pelagius and his followers. [2] It had condemned the errors of the Pelagians, who attributed man's good works to his own free will and not to God's gratuitous help, and who, even where they allowed the activity of grace, conceived of it only as an exterior help, and, at any rate, proportioned to man's previous merits. But difficulties had arisen in the minds of Augustine's disciples even during his lifetime on some points in his teaching. [3] Two statements of his aroused surprise, if not opposition, among the monks of Hadrumetum in North Africa. He had written that the beginning of all good works comes from grace and not from man, and that final perseverance is a gift of God and not the result of man's efforts. Set against the background of St. Augustine's views on the Fall and based on his rigid conceptions on predestination and reprobation, according to which God seemed to choose some men for the revelation of His mercy and to leave others for the manifestation of His Justice,[4] these teachings seemed to them to endanger, or render useless, man's striving for virtue.

When consulted on the matter, St. Augustine gave his answer in two treatises. In the *De gratia et libero arbitrio*[5] he established the fact that man's free will remains untouched, and is rather perfected by grace; and he proved the reality of both free will and grace from the Scriptures, without, however, attempting to reconcile the two, as in later times theology would do. In the *De correptione et gratia*[6] he explained the nature, action, and distribution of grace, seen in the light of our historical state: the human race after original sin is a *massa damnationis* out of which God's mercy freely chooses His predestined elect. Augustine's explanations apparently satisfied the Hadrumetan monks, but they were to lead to new controversies in the monastic centres of Southern Gaul. There the opposition of the *Massilienses*, the monks of Marseilles, to Augustine's teaching developed into a heterodox position which their opponents were to style the *reliquiae Pelagianorum* and which was to be known as Semi-Pelagianism only many centuries later.[7]

The history of this reaction against St. Augustine's teaching on predestination[8] and on its connexion with the doctrine of grace falls into two periods of heated controversy.[9] The first of these controversies, prepared and set in motion during the last years of St. Augustine's lifetime, flared up violently almost immediately after his death in 430. It took place in some monasteries of Southern Gaul, at Marseilles and Lerins. The chief defender of Augustine's doctrine on grace against the new error was St. Prosper of Aquitaine, a layman who was connected with the

monasteries, a faithful follower and occasional corre-
spondent of St. Augustine.[10] His *Epistola ad Augustinum* [11]
together with another letter to St. Augustine written by
Hilary, a friend of his,[12] in which they exposed to their
master the novel teachings of the monks and asked for
advice and direction, occasioned the first and last direct
intervention of the seventy-five year old bishop of Hippo
in the Semi-Pelagian controversy: the two books known
as *De praedestinatione sanctorum* and *De dono persever-
antiae.*[13]

Originally two parts of one treatise, the first dealt with
the problem of the inception of faith in our souls, the
second exposed the doctrine of the gift of perseverance.
In both St. Augustine showed how the Semi-Pelagians,
though protesting that they would have nothing to do
with Pelagius' heresy, yet, unless they agreed to attribute
the beginning of faith and final perseverance to grace,
did away with the gratuitousness of grace, and thus went
over into Pelagius' camp.[14] On the Semi-Pelagian side
the chief opponents to Augustinism were Cassian, abbot
of the Marseilles monastery of St. Victor and author of
the famous *Conferences,*[15] and St. Vincent of Lerins who
wrote the *Commonitorium* [16] in a strongly anti-Augustin-
ian tone, and was probably connected with the composition and circulation of the pamphlet known as the *Obiec-
tiones Vincentianae.*[17] The first phase of the controversies
ended soon after Cassian's death in 435, but not without
a partial withdrawal of the Augustinians, expressed in
the *Capitula, seu praeteritorum Sedis Apostolicae episcoporum auctoritates de gratia Dei.* This Roman document, drawn up by St. Prosper before 441-442, states the
points of Catholic doctrine that were involved in the

controversy, but it leaves out the deeper and more obscure questions.[18]

A period of relative calm ensued which gave St. Prosper an opportunity for a quiet and peaceful review of the whole dispute. The *De vocatione* was the fruit of this study. Whether it was, in spite of its moderate and conciliatory tone, the occasion for reviving the old controversies or not, a new outburst of anti-Augustinism soon followed when Faustus of Riez, first a monk and later abbot at Lerins, and from about 462, bishop of Riez, published his *De gratia Dei*.[19] After repudiating the old Pelagian error and affirming his faith in God's grace, he restated the two Semi-Pelagian theses. In the process of man's salvation the initiative belongs to man, otherwise his free will would be destroyed; and so, too, for the same reason, does final perseverance. Incidentally, against the unnamed author of the *De vocatione*, he insists on an interpretation of God's universal salvific will that practically eliminates predestination.[20] Meeting with little opposition in France (St. Prosper was no longer there; perhaps he was dead by then), but faced with a decided opponent in North Africa, St. Fulgentius of Ruspe,[21] the fate of this last phase of Semi-Pelagianism was, after long-drawn-out wrangles and protracted delays caused by the barbarian invasions in Southern Europe, finally sealed at the Council of Orange in 529,[22] where St. Caesarius of Arles [23] was the leading figure. The decisions of this council, particularly its *capitula* 9 to 25, were mainly taken from St. Prosper's *Liber sententiarum ex S. Augustino delibatarum*.[24]

The *De vocatione* thus originated during the period of quiet between the two critical phases of the Semi-Pelagian controversies. About this all patristic scholars agree.[25] The question, however, of its authorship has been disputed,[26] especially since the second half of the seventeenth century. Up to that date the traditional view, in accord with the manuscript tradition and with the medieval authors who quote it under St. Prosper's name, held Prosper to be the author. Little credence could be given to a manifestly erroneous opinion, found in some manuscripts and accepted by a few editors in the fifteenth and sixteenth centuries, which attributed the *De vocatione* to St. Ambrose.[27] The anachronism is evident, as St. Ambrose had died before either Pelagianism or Semi-Pelagianism were born.[28]

But when Quesnel, who was editing the works of St. Leo the Great, claimed the authorship of the book for that saint, on the strength of internal evidence revealed in certain Leonine ideas and expressions only,[29] then was the traditional opinion shaken. Quesnel's own opinion found little favour with others, but he succeeded in casting a doubt on the accepted view that St. Prosper was the author. Thus his opponent in the matter, J. Antelmi,[30] while defending St. Prosper's authorship, supported the opinion which Quesnel had put forward and which Du Pin [31] was later to spread with considerable success—that the author, in order to cover up his attempt at reconciling Augustinism and Semi-Pelagianism, purposely remained anonymous. In the face of all these differences of opinions and arguments one thing seemed clear to the Ballerini brothers [32] when in 1756 they re-edited the *De vocatione* among the works of St. Leo, namely, that the question of its authorship remained uncertain. It is this solution, or this lack of solution, which was the more commonly accepted view of patristic scholars down to our own day.[33]

Some twenty years ago, however, a new attempt was made, and not without success, to re-establish the formerly accepted authorship of St. Prosper. Dom M. C. Cappuyns has proposed [34] the following arguments to prove that the *De vocatione* is a work of St. Prosper, and to refute at the same time all other opinions:

1) The manuscript tradition, apart from the few references to St. Ambrose which need no serious consideration, unanimously points out St. Prosper as the author. This can be vouched for from the ninth to the fifteenth century.[35] Literary attestations in favour of St. Prosper confirm this tradition. In 852 the *De vocatione* is quoted in favour of Augustinism under Prosper's name by Ratramnus of Corbia; [36] and a little later by his adversary Hincmar of Rheims,[37] against the Augustinian doctrine of predestination. If we take into account that St. Prosper's works, except for one letter to St. Augustine, have not come down to us in manuscripts dated before the ninth century,[38] and that tradition is unanimous in naming St. Prosper, we have to discard definitely the hypothesis of an intentional anonymity.[39]

2) The teaching of the *De vocatione is* identical with that of St. Prosper on practically all points of doctrine.[40]

3) The literary procedure is the same: similar expressions, similar ways of developing ideas.[41]

4) One particular and revealing indication is found in the Scripture quotations. The same versions of the Scripture (Vulgate or older texts) are used in the *De vocatione* and in St. Prosper, and, what is more striking, combining the new and old versions for the same passages.[42]

Cappuyns concludes: "Who can the author be who thinks, reasons, writes exactly like Prosper? Who else but Prosper himself?" [43] Further, he completes his proof by answering all arguments Quesnel had advanced in favour of St. Leo. He shows that Quesnel's attribution of authorship to Leo rests on internal evidence only; that it goes against all the external evidence of the manuscript and literary attestations; that it is made improbable by the divergent mentality of the Doctor of the Incarnation, eminently practical and clear-minded, and interested ever so little in the subtleties of the Gallic controversies. A close examination of the parallel texts on which Quesnel based his conclusion, reveals a similarity which is more apparent than real, and which in every case leaves room for differences in the ideas. That the similarity pointed out does not postulate an identity of authorship, can be sufficiently shown by the influence exercised by St. Leo on the author of the *De vocatione*. And this influence was to be expected considering that St. Prosper at the time of writing the treatise lived in Rome, at the papal court, as secretary to St. Leo. [44]

We may, then, align ourselves with a number of patristic scholars [45] and safely accept Cappuyns' conclusion that St. Prosper's authorship of the *De vocatione* is historically established.

If we admit that St. Prosper is the author of our treatise, it is imperative to find a place for it in his literary and doctrinal evolution. We know but little about his person, except that he was a layman of Southern Gaul, connected with the monasteries there, especially at the time of the first Semi-Pelagian controversies, and that he left his home country for Rome and the papal court shortly after Cassian's death in 435.[46] His literary work, however—poetical, theological, and historical—is sufficiently well-known and dated.[47] Students of St. Prosper are agreed in perceiving a progress and development in his doctrinal positions, but there are different opinions as to the extent of this evolution.[48] The question in dispute is this: did St. Prosper who was a loyal disciple of St. Augustine and a staunch defender of his doctrine, remain faithful to all the ideas of his master on grace and predestination, or is there a real difference between the works of his youth, where, in fact, he faithfully echoes St. Augustine, and those of his later years? [49] All agree that even at the time of writing the *De vocatione* St. Prosper remained thoroughly Augustinian, penetrated with the ideas and moulded on the spirit of the Doctor of Grace, of whose teachings and words we find reminiscences in nearly every chapter of our treatise.[50] All seem to think that there has been an evolution in his rigidly formulated Augustinism, particularly in the question of predestination, where he toned down some of his master's exaggerated expressions. This evolution, according to some, goes even further than the bare expressions—it affects his ideas as well. The point is not without importance for the understanding of the *De vocatione*.

With Cappuyns,[51] who sees in St. Prosper the first representative of medieval Augustinism, we may divide his literary activity over three periods of unequal length. The first period, of rigid Augustinism and strict fidelity to St. Augustine's teachings on predestination and grace, extends to the year 432. He holds the doctrine of absolute predestination and non-predestination, and of a restricted salvific will; and he links the gratuitousness of grace with predestination. The second period, 433-435, covers his first concessions to the Semi-Pelagian positions. He concedes that the salvific will is universal and explains the negative counterpart of predestination, that is, reprobation, as mere prescience of evil. God does not predestine any one to evil, He only foreknows it. But no explicit distinction is as yet made between the Catholic doctrine and Augustinian teaching. In the third period we find him making the great concessions to his adversaries. The progressive element in his doctrinal position is the conscious distinction he makes between the authentic teaching of the Church and the private opinions of the Doctors, and even of St. Augustine. In the matter of predestination and grace this means the dissociation of the gratuitousness of grace from the Augustinian views on predestination. About these latter St. Prosper takes a more independent attitude. Consequently, he is able to lay greater stress on the universalism of God's salvific will. The *De vocatione* belongs to this third period.[52]

Our treatise examines the problem of the salvation of all men from a double aspect. If God's salvific will is universal—and of this there can be no doubt—how is it that many are not saved, or, as the author prefers to view it, how is it that many do not receive the grace that saves (Book One)?[53] And inversely, if many are not saved or do not receive the grace that saves, how can there really be in God a universal salvific will (Book Two)?

The problem is difficult, and, especially in Prosper's time, it was a delicate one to tackle. St. Prosper proposes to explain the doctrine of God's universal salvific will. But it so happened that St. Augustine had not, or, at any rate, had not clearly, taught a universalist doctrine about God's will of salvation; rather, he had repeatedly interpreted the

Scripture texts about God's will to save men, in a restrictive sense.[54] On the other hand, the Semi-Pelagians, Prosper's opponents, forcefully stressed the universality of God's salvific will in order to drive home their point regarding the initiative of man's free will in the work of salvation.[55] St. Prosper had therefore to steer a middle course between these two extremes. Against Semi-Pelagianism he had to assert the absolute gratuitousness of grace, but in such wise as to safeguard a real universal salvific will. On the other hand, in spite of St. Augustine's teaching, he had to maintain the universalism of God's will to save men, without, however, impairing the gratuitousness of grace; this gratuitousness he held, with Augustine, to be the Catholic doctrine.

Did he succeed in avoiding the danger on both sides and synthesize the complete gratuitousness of grace with God's universal salvific will? [56] To effect this synthesis, one way alone was open, namely, to disconnect the gratuitous character of grace from the Augustinian doctrine on predestination.[57] Predestination of the elect only, such as St. Augustine was commonly understood to have taught, and a universal will to save all men do not go hand in hand. St. Prosper certainly tried to separate these two doctrines and did so effectively up to a point. A glance at the contents of each book will enable us to judge about the matter.

God wills all men to be saved. Yet many are not saved and do not receive the grace that actually saves. Why? (1). From the threefold degree of man's will, animal, natural, and spiritual, it appears that all initiative for good comes from grace (2-8). But the universal salvific will as taught in Scripture can be understood in the sense of a specified or restricted totality (9-12); the mysterious reason of its restriction remains unknown to us (13 f.). Saving grace, however, is wholly gratuitous (15), as is clear in the case of children dying before the age of reason (16) and from death-bed conversions (17). It is given without any preceding merit (18) or any effective initiative of nature for good (19). Yet there is a divine salvific will for all (20), though the reason why God chose Israel and left aside the Gentiles, remains a mystery (21). This, however, is certain: the chosen ones are chosen without any merit of their own (22), for all gifts of grace are totally gratuitous (23 f.). Why they are given to one and not to another is a mystery which we cannot fathom (25).[58]

What, then, is the answer of Book One to the first aspect of the problem: how is it that, in spite of God's universal salvific will, not all men are saved? Because they do not all receive the grace that actually saves. For this, however, no one can rightly blame God, since grace is a gratuitous gift. We cannot know why it is given to some and not to some others.

We may consider this answer to be rather unsatisfactory. St. Prosper's insistence on the gratuitousness of grace appears to be beside the point.[59] As he himself asks in the first chapter, why does God not give all men the gift without which no one can be saved, if He really wants all to be saved? Book One does not give the answer. For St. Prosper, too, the problem is not solved. He has, no doubt, maintained the gratuitousness of grace; but has he not sacrificed the universalism of the salvific will? Inevitably the objection which arises is the one formulated in the last chapter: if many are not saved because they do not receive the grace that saves, how, then, can we believe—as we must—that there is in God a really universal salvific will? The answer to this difficulty is the central theme of Book Two.

It begins by stating three points that are certain in the matter: God wills all men to be saved; knowledge of the truth and salvation come from grace; God's judgments are impenetrable (1). Scripture tells us that God wills all men to be saved (2), but we do not know how this will works, why He delays to call some (3). Still, there always was a general call addressed to all men and a special election for Israel (4). Even among the Gentiles there were some specially chosen (5). In fact, there are differences in the graces of God (6) which are not due to previous merits (7), since all merit originates from grace (8); differences of which we cannot and need not know the reason (9). The fact remains that God's mercy is shown to all (10) and spreads out its gifts in the course of time (11). Without these gifts free will leads only to evil (12). Even for the wicked there was, and is, divine grace (13-15), for Christ died for all (16). The fruits of His Redemption are to be applied to men at the appointed time (17) as they also were in former ages (18). At all times, therefore, God's salvific will was universal (19). If you bring up the case of infants who die without baptism (20), St. Prosper answers by saying that they are not treated unjustly (21); God's judgments are just (22); these children, too, received the general grace in the call of their parents (23); their case only serves to bring out both God's justice and grace (24). Here, then, is the solution: God's salvific will provides a general grace for all men, but a special grace for some (25). It is grace that produces in men both the good will and the consent to good (26 f.), but in such a way that they remain free (28). The universal salvific will is being fulfilled every day (29). Prosper briefly repeats what is certain in the matter in question (30 = 1). At all times grace has been given to all men but in different measure, not due to their merits, but to God's hidden judgments (31 f.). The elect, however, are certainly saved (33), their good works and prayers being a factor in the work of their salvation (34-36). The fact of their election remains unknown during their stay on earth (37).

Why, then, can we say that there is in God a universal salvific will, in spite of the fact that many are lost? The answer of Book Two is: God's real will to save all men is shown by the general grace He gives to all, with no one left out—no, not even the infants; but His special grace that leads to actual salvation He freely and gratuitously bestows only on the elect who remain free to collaborate with grace and who alone are actually saved. As to the reason of this discrimination in God's gifts to men, this is a mystery not known to men.

The originality of St. Prosper's *De vocatione* in solving the problem of the salvation of all mankind lies in this idea of a general grace given to all men. He has been the first to state this in explicit terms. He may have found the germ of the idea in St. Augustine,[60] or he may have obtained it from St. Leo,[61] but the clear expression of it is his original contribution. We have, therefore, to consider it more closely. His explanation of the universal salvific will may be synthesized as follows:

God wills all men to be saved, even the children who die before baptism. The proof and expression of this will is the general grace He refuses to no one, not even to the children. Yet not all are actually saved, because they do not receive the special graces that lead to actual salvation.

The general grace which is given to all comprises two elements, an exterior one and an interior one. The exterior help is the testimony of the created things which reveal to men their Maker. The interior help, which is like the spirit of this preaching opposed to the letter, is the illumination of the heart by God. When men accept this grace and co-operate with it as they can and should, they receive further special graces. These are necessary for salvation, but, apparently, are withheld by God only when men reject them or reject the previous graces offered them. The special graces are of two kinds; or rather, they lead to two different results: either to a temporary practice of virtue as in the case of the just who do not persevere in grace, through their own fault, for God abandons no one who does not first turn away from Him; or to final perseverance, in the case of the elect who are foreknown as such by God.[62]

Children also receive the general grace, in their parents. If the parents co-operate with the general grace they receive—and even infidels receive it—then they will also be given the special graces that are needed to come to the faith, and their children also will be brought to what is for them the only concrete form of the special grace, the sacrament of baptism.[63]

In the history of the economy of grace we see that the Gentiles always received the general grace in the testimony of created things. Some of them responded to it and they received further special graces that led them to actual salvation. Israel, God's chosen people, was given the same general grace, and besides, the special graces of the Law and the Prophets—special exterior graces which, however, did not save all of them but only those who accepted them and received also the necessary interior graces (*for the letter killeth* . . .). Ever since Christ came into the world and saved mankind, the special grace of the Gospel is offered to all. It has not reached all the Gentiles yet, but it is destined to do so and will do so in the appointed time. All who accept this special exterior grace and are given the corresponding interior grace come to justification, and if they are the elect, to final perseverance and salvation.

What are we to think of this solution? Does it give the answer as to why, in spite of God's universal salvific will, not all men are saved; and inversely, why God's will to save mankind is really universal although many are not actually saved? We may notice how St. Prosper in proposing his theory is struggling to break away from the influence of the Augustinian predestination or election doctrine.[64] Owing to his inability to free himself fully from it, his idea of the general grace, universally given to all, fails to solve the problem. His solution appears purely nominal. For a will of salvation can hardly be called real when it is expressed only in a non-saving grace; the general grace is actually such. No salvation of any one individual can take place without special graces, additional to the general one, and these are not given to all. If it were clearly said that the only reason why these special graces are not given to some, is because they themselves refuse them,[65] then the proposed solution would in fact mean a great step forward in the right direction. Unfortunately, this idea is rather insinuated than clearly stated. The idea of the divine election which haunts our author prevents him from taking this step frankly. His attempt at reconciling a universalist doctrine of the divine salvific will with a theory of election that remains essentially the same as Augustinian predestination, may then in reality come to little more than "a good intention." [66]

Yet from another point of view the *De vocatione* holds an important place in the history of Augustinism and of St. Augustine's influence on Catholic theology. It is an evident desire and an effective attempt to tone down Augustine's rigid expressions and views on predestination. This may be observed not only in the terminology by the conspicuous absence of all "predestinational" terms, which are avoided, seemingly, of set purpose, but also in the ideas themselves, especially when drawn out in relief. [67] God's universal salvific will is stressed incomparably more than it had ever been by St. Augustine. Quite certainly it is the awareness of this change in outlook and in conception together with a sense of reverence for the memory of the Doctor of Grace which prompts St. Prosper to omit any explicit reference to him in this treatise. Human freedom which remains intact under the action of grace is brought into greater relief here than it was in Augustine's works. The gratuitousness of grace is no less stressed than it had been by Augustine, but here it is explained without explicit connection with predestination. This latter, called by Prosper election, and chiefly stressed as God's eternal and infallible foreknowledge of His elect, comes in only as the answer to the mysterious *why* of God's discriminating choice.

Perhaps this change of viewpoint, with its consequent

shifting of the stress laid now on ideas which St. Augustine may have known, but left in the background of his general outlook, constitutes St. Prosper's chief emancipation from rigid Augustinism. Besides this point, some passing intuitions that are hardly exploited by him, imply a real beginning of a doctrine which would later be developed in a more boldly universalistic sense; as, for example, the mention (2.5) of the grace that singled out the elect from the Gentiles. We must not overstress this and similar elements of progress in a direction which would lead to our present-day unquestioned view that all men receive sufficient graces to be saved if they wish to be saved. All the same, the *De vocatione* constituted at the time when it was written a definite attempt to get loose from Augustinian particularism in the doctrine of the salvation of mankind.[68] It was certainly partially successful, and due to the influence it was to exert in the early Middle Ages,[69] it prepared the way for further progress in the same direction.

ʃ ʃ ʃ

The text from which the present translation was made is that of the Ballerini, as found in the second volume of their edition of St. Leo, Venice, 1756, cols. 167-250.[70] This seems to be the best among the printed texts of the *De vocatione,* and is better than Mangeant's edition, Paris, 1711,[71] which was reprinted in Migne's *Patrologia latina* 51, from the re-edition of Venice, 1827. As, however, the Ballerini text is more rarely found than the one reprinted by Migne, we shall point out its different readings whenever they affect the meaning.[72]

As to modern translations, we have been able to use

the three-century-old French version published in Paris in 1649 by Père Antoine Girard, under the title, *Saint Prosper, disciple de Saint Augustin, De la Vocation des Gentils, où la Doctrine Catholique de la liberté et de la Grâce est déclarée contre les erreurs des Hérétiques et de ceux qui favorisent leur party.*[73]  No other more recent translation of the work seems to have been made.  To our knowledge none is found in the English, German, Italian, or other collections of the works of the Fathers.  At all events, the present translation appears to be the first English version of St. Prosper's treatise on *The Call of All Nations.*

# DIVISION

### BOOK TWO

# BOOK ONE

## CHAPTER 1

*The author states the theme of this book and shows the
error of those who hold that to predicate
grace means to deny free will.*

A great and difficult problem has long been debated
among the defenders of free will and the advocates of the
grace of God.[1] The point at issue is whether God wills
all men to be saved; and since this cannot be denied,[2]
the question arises, why the will of the Almighty is not
realized. When this is said to happen because of the
will of men, grace seems to be ruled out; and if grace is
a reward for merit, it is clearly not a gift but something
due to men.[3] But then the question again arises: why
is this gift, without which no one can attain salvation, not
conferred on all, by Him who wills all to be saved? Hence,
there is no end to discussions in either camp so long as
they make no distinction between what can be known
and what remains hidden.[4]

On this conflict of opinions I shall endeavour,[5] with
the Lord's help, to investigate what restraint and modera-
tion we ought to maintain in our views. I shall apply to
this study my meagre talents in a matter where my own
convictions are, I think, moderate. Thus, if in writing on
this subject I can avoid all that is offensive or wrong, it
may prove useful, not only for us but also for others, to
have found out a limit where our inquiry should stop.[6]

First of all, then, we have to study the operations of the human will in its different degrees.[7] Some people set up an untenable cleavage between this will of men and God's grace, holding that by predicating grace one denies free will.[8] They do not notice that it could be objected equally well that they deny grace when they consider the latter not as leading, but as following, the human will.[9] For if the will is suppressed when it is not the source of true virtues, then also is grace eliminated when it is not the cause of merits.[10] But let us now, with Christ's help, begin our treatise.

CHAPTER 2

*Every human soul has a will of some kind, whether it be animal or natural or spiritual.*

Every human soul, as far as we can know it from experience, is endowed with a will manifesting itself in some manner or other.[11] It desires what is pleasing and turns away from what displeases. With regard to its natural impulses now weakened by the infection of the first sin, this will is of two kinds, either animal or natural. But when God's grace is present, a third kind is added by the gift of the Spirit.[12] The will then becomes spiritual, and thanks to this higher impulse, it rules all its affections, from wheresoever they may arise, according to the law of a higher wisdom.[13]

## CHAPTER 3

### *The animal will.*

The animal will,[14] which we may also call carnal, does not rise above the impulse that is born of the bodily senses, as in the case of infants. Although these do not have the use of reason, yet they show that they desire some things and do not want others. When they see, hear, smell, taste, touch, they love what pleases them and hate what hurts them. Now, what else is love but desire? Or what else is hatred but aversion? They, too, have therefore a will of their own. This will may be inexperienced and unable to foresee or to deliberate, but it likes to be busy about objects that flatter the animal senses—until rational nature wakes up to life in them, when the functions of the body are more developed, and is stirred to use the service of its limbs, not at another's bidding but according to its own ruling.

## CHAPTER 4

### *The natural will. The only compensation it offers is earthly glory, even when through God's gift it rises to a higher wisdom.*

From this animal will, which is the only one found in those adults who are insane and remain deprived of the use of reason, man rises to the level of the natural will.[15] Though at this stage the will can, before it is guided by the Spirit of God, raise itself above its animal impulses, still, as long as it does not share in divine charity, it busies itself with earthly and perishable things. When led by it at this level, human hearts do not, it is true, undergo the shameful slavery of bodily pleasures, but rule their desires according to the laws of justice and probity. They do not, however, merit any higher reward than earthly glory. Although they succeed in leading the present life in a becoming manner, still they do not reap the reward of eternal happiness.[16] For they do not refer their righteous actions and good endeavours to the praise and honour of Him who gave them the power of actually fostering a higher wisdom and of gaining greater glory than others.[17] Some, in fact, have applied their minds not only to the practice of the useful arts and to the study of the liberal sciences, but also to the quest of the supreme Good. They clearly saw and understood *the invisible things of God by the things that are made.*[18] But, failing to give thanks to God and acknowledge Him as the author of this their faculty, *they professed themselves to be wise;*[19] that is, they gloried not in God but in themselves, as if they had reached the knowledge of truth through their own efforts of reasoning. They *became vain in their thoughts,*[20] and what they had gained in the light of God's grace, they lost again in the blindness of their pride. They fell back from the heavenly light into their own darkness, that is, from the changeless and eternal Good to their own fickle and corruptible nature.[21]

Such men, therefore, return to self-love. They are so pleased with themselves, that whatever they judge praise-worthy in their own persons, they do not refer to God's gifts; they claim it as their own merit and attribute it

to the efforts of their own wills. Consequently, they
remain below the level of the spiritual will. They possess
in themselves nothing to lead them on to eternal life, for
they actually begin to spoil in their own hearts those very
natural gifts of God, and they pass from a rightful use of
them to the practice of unnumbered vices.[22]


## CHAPTER 5

*All the Gentiles have received in things created
the precepts of the Law so that their
idolatry is unwarrantable.*

It is written that *when the Most High divided the
nations, as He dispersed the sons of Adam, He appointed
the bounds of the nations according to the number of the
angels of God, and His people became the Lord's portion
Jacob, the lot of His inheritance Israel.*[23] It is also written
that the Lord spoke to Israel: *You will be holy before me,
because I am holy the Lord your God, who separated you
from all nations to be mine.*[24] It is further written in the
Book of Esther, Mardochai speaking: *I give Thee thanks,
Lord, because Thou hast wrought new signs and wonders,
as have not happened among the nations, dividing the
whole world into two parts; one didst Thou choose as
Thy own people, leaving the other for the Gentiles.*[25]
Paul, too, and Barnabas said: *We also are mortals, men
like unto you, preaching to you to be converted . . . to the
living God who made the heaven and the earth and the
sea and all things that are in them; who in times past*

*suffered all nations to walk in their own ways.*[26] These and many similar statements are found in the infallible Scripture. Yet according to the same Scripture we believe and devoutly confess that never was mankind as a whole without the care of Divine Providence.[27] And, though Providence led the people it had chosen to a right way of conduct through special ordinances, it did not, nevertheless, withhold the gifts of its goodness from any nation among men. They manifestly have been taught the pronouncements of the Prophets and the precepts of the Law by the things created [28]—the services they received from them and the lessons they gathered from them.[29] Hence, they had no excuse when they made into gods the very gifts of God and when they turned into objects of worship that which was created for their use.[30]

CHAPTER 6

*Without divine grace, the more keenly the will is intent on action, the more quickly does it run into sin, because it does not live for God's glory.*

Even the nation which the Lord had separated unto Himself from among all nations, would have fallen completely into this wickedness, had not the design of His mercy taken care to support His elect who were ever stumbling. The pages of the Old Testament are full of the story of Israel's defections, in order that it may appear clearly that it was always due only to divine grace when not all the people fell away from the Lord.[31] Thus human nature, vitiated in the first man's sin, is always inclined, even when surrounded with God's mercies, with His precepts and aids, towards a degenerate will, to surrender to which means sin.[32] This will, then, is unsettled, uncertain, unsteadfast, unwise, weak to accomplish, quick to risk, blind in desire, conceited when honoured, agitated with cares, restless with suspicions, more desirous of glory than of virtue, more solicitous of a good reputation than of a good conscience, and through all its experiences still more unhappy when enjoying what is coveted than when deprived of it. It has of its own nothing but a readiness to fall; for a fickle will which is not ruled by the changeless will of God, runs the more quickly into sin the more keenly it is bent on action.[33]

As long, then, as man takes pleasure in what displeases God, his will remains on a natural plane, because even when his action is morally good, his life remains bad if he does not live for God's glory.[34] For this is the chief characteristic of the devout, that they glory in the Lord and do not love themselves except in God. Hence, only they love themselves well who love in their persons the works of God. Obviously, God also loves in us what He himself has wrought in us, and He hates what is not His work. If, then, we love God's work in us, we rightly love in ourselves the will for good which surely would not be lovable if it were not God's creation.[35] But who is the man except he be of a bad will, who would not love in himself the good will, which is the first plant of the heavenly Husbandman? When the Truth says, *Every plant which my heavenly Father hath not planted shall be rooted up,*[36] it is clear that whatever is not to be rooted up was planted by the Father. Now, good will is the first seed of all virtues. When it relies on its source, it rests on the eternal and unchanging will and thus truly becomes spiritual.[37] For *he who is joined to God, is one spirit.*[38] Then, through the communion of the Illuminator with the illuminated, of the Justifier with the justified, of the Ruler with the ruled all action is referred to one end,[39] and this same action thus referred to one end belongs to both: from God cannot be taken away what He has given, nor from man what he has received.[40]

### CHAPTER 7

*When a man is converted to God, no new substance is created in him, but his own which was spoiled is remade. Nothing is taken away from him but vice, and his former will is set right.*

This seems to be the place to put the question: When a man is converted to a will disposed to do good, is then the will that was in him set right, or does he receive a new will which he did not have before and which is the reverse of his former one?[41] To make this clearer, let us make the effort to look into the matter more thoroughly.

All of us have been created in the first man without any blemish and we have all lost the integrity of our nature through the sin of the same first man. Hence followed mortality, hence the manifold corruption of body and mind, ignorance and difficulty, useless cares, unlawful desires, sacrilegious aberrations, vain fears, harmful love, unholy pleasures, blamable designs, and as great a host

of woes as of sins. With these and other evils assailing
human nature, with faith lost, hope abandoned, the intellect blinded, the will enslaved,[42] no one finds in himself
the means of a restoration. Although some tried, guided
by their natural reason, to resist vices, the life of decency
they led here on earth was sterile. They did not acquire
true virtues and attain eternal happiness. Without worship of the true God even what has the appearance of
virtue is sin. No one can please God without God.[43] But
he who does not please God, whom will he please but
himself and the devil?

When man was robbed by the devil, he was not deprived
of his will but of the righteousness of his will.[44] For man
could not be thrust down from the state of innocence
unless he sinned wilfully. Thus his nature which was
good has been infected by an evil quality;[45] and the soul's
aspiration which can never be without some love, that
is, without some will, has not lost its power of desiring
but it has changed its affections. It now embraces in
desire what it should have rejected by reason. When,
therefore, a man returns to God, the Scripture word
applies to him, *a wind that goeth and returneth not,*[46]
because if God did not convert him, he would not return;[47]
and when he becomes a new cast and a new creature,[48]
then no new substance is created in him, but his own
which was shaken is restored. Nothing else is taken away
from him but the blemish which he did not have by
nature.

## CHAPTER 8

*Grace repairs God's work in such a manner as not to take
away free will but rather to heal it by itself.*

In Adam our nature existed without blemish, but
he by his wilful disobedience incurred many evils and
transmitted them to his posterity in whom they were to
multiply more and more. The victory over these evils
and their utter destruction only springs from the grace of
the Saviour who restores His own work with His own
labour.[49] For, as the Apostle John says, *For this purpose
the Son of God appeared, that He might destroy the
works of the devil.*[50] He it is who breaks the chains of the
prisoner, He clothes the nakedness of the robbed man,
He heals the injuries of the wounded, but all this in such a
manner that what He works in him is also effected by man
himself.[51] He indeed cannot risk to fight against his enemy
without a protector. He has to wage war against one who
once defeated him. He should, therefore, not trust in
his own strength which, even when it was unimpaired,
did not hold out; but let him seek victory through the
One who alone is unconquerable and who brought victory
to all.

And if he does seek victory, he should not doubt that
he has received this very desire of seeking it from Him
whom he is seeking.[52] And he should not think that,
because he is led by the Spirit of God,[53] he no longer has
free will.[54] This he did not lose even when he wilfully
surrendered himself to the devil. The devil perverted his
judgment that goes with the will, but did not take it

from him. What was not taken away [55] by the one who inflicted a wound is still less destroyed by the One who comes to heal. He heals the wound, He does not set aside nature. But what was lost in nature cannot be restored except by its Author; in whose sight what was lost in nature did not perish.[56] He is eternal wisdom, eternal truth, eternal goodness, eternal justice, He is, in short, the eternal light of all virtues, and all that is virtue is God.[57] Unless He works in us, we cannot be partakers of any virtue. For indeed without this Good nothing is good, without this Light nothing is bright, without this Wisdom nothing is wise, without this Justice nothing is right.[58] For the Lord says through the mouth of Isaias, *I am, I am the Lord, and there is no one besides me who saves;* [59] and Jeremias says, *I know, O Lord, that the way of a man is not in him; neither is it in a man to direct his way.*[60]

Mortal man, born according to the flesh from a source that was cursed in Adam, cannot come to the spiritual dignity of the new birth except through the guidance of the Holy Spirit. Indeed, he cannot even foster any desire for it as long as he has not received from God the ardour of this desire,[61] about which the Lord says, *I am come to cast fire on the earth, and what will I, but that it be burning?* [62] That fire is the love of God which a lover of the world cannot conceive in his enslaved heart. He is filled with the love of vain things, and even if he could escape these to some extent, and, rising above temporal and visible goods, attain through his own understanding the eternal and invisible ones; [63] even if he could renounce the worship of idols and give up the adoration of heaven and earth and all the created things of this world; [64] even so he would not conceive the faith and the love of Christ, because he would be upset by His lowliness. He would not with his own insight overcome the scandal of our Lord's nativity and death. For, as the wisdom of the world resists the wisdom of God, thus blinding the pride of the self-conceited, so *it pleased God by the foolishness of our preaching to save them that believe.*[65] Hence, those who are made arrogant by their worldly learning, think that the Cross of Christ is something to be laughed at rather than adored; and the higher a man rises in the attainments of the human sciences, the more he scorns the humility and feebleness of our preaching.

No wonder either, that pagan philosophy opposes the Gospel of the Cross of Christ, when Jewish learning also resists it. We conclude that neither the learned nor the illiterate of whatever race or rank come to God led by human reason; but every man who is converted to God is first stirred by God's grace.[66] For man is no light unto himself, nor can he inflame his own heart with a ray of his own light. If Saint John than whom no son of men was greater,[67] *was not the light* because he did not shine with his own brightness, but had received the power to enlighten others from the true Light *which enlighteneth every man that cometh into this world:* what man is there who would give up so many conflicting opinions, so many constraining habits, so many inveterate prejudices, relying only on his own judgment and helped solely by the spoken word of a teacher? Grace would then consist only in the exterior hearing of the doctrine and the whole of a man's faith would spring from his own will.[68] If such were the case, there would be no difference between grace and the Law; and the spirit of forgiveness would enliven no one if *the letter that kills* remained. For indeed the Law commands things to be done or avoided, but it does not help one to do or to avoid them.[69] Its rigour is complied with not out of free choice but out of fear. But the Lord with a view not to destroy but to fulfil the Law,[70] through the help of His grace, made the command of the Law effective, and through the abundance of His clemency lifted its penal sanction so that He might not avenge sin with punishments, but destroy it through forgiveness.[71]

That is why the adulterous woman whom the Law prescribed to be stoned, was set free by Him with truth and grace, when the avengers of the Law frightened with the state of their own conscience had left the trembling guilty woman to the judgment of Him who had come *to seek and save what was lost.*[72] And for that reason He, bowing down—that is, stooping down to our human level and intent on the work of our reformation—*wrote with His finger on the ground,*[73] in order to repeal the Law of the commandments with the decrees of His grace [74] and to reveal Himself as the One who had said, *I will give my laws in their understanding and I will write them in their heart.*[75] This indeed He does every day when He infuses His will into the hearts of those who are called, and when with the pen [76] of the Holy Spirit the Truth mercifully rewrites on the pages of their souls all that the devil enviously falsified.

Whenever, then, the word of God enters into the ears of the body through the ministry of the preachers, the action of the divine power fuses with the sound of a human voice,[77] and He who is the inspirer of the preacher's office is also the strength of the hearer's heart. Then the food of the word becomes sweet to the soul; the darkness of old is expelled by the new light; the interior eye is freed from the cataracts of the ancient error; the soul passes from one will to another,[78] and although the will that is driven out lingers on for a while, yet the newborn one claims for itself all that is better in man, so that the law of sin and the law of God do not dwell in the same way and together in the same man.[79] And then, whilst *the flesh lusteth against the spirit and the spirit also resists the desires of the flesh,*[80] the tempter ventures to ambush man through exterior objects; but the mind strong with God's help prevails. For, obviously, there are occasions for struggle and these serve the great profit of the faithful: their weakness is buffeted that their holiness may not yield to pride.[81] Hence, too, the Apostle says: *Lest in the greatness of the revelations I should be exalted, there was given me . . . an angel of Satan to buffet me. For which thing thrice I besought the Lord that it might depart from me, but He said to me: My grace is sufficient for thee, for power is made perfect in infirmity.*[82]

Let, then, the Lord seek His image;[83] let the Good Shepherd find His erring sheep and not disdain to bear it, sick and tired for long of the trackless wilds, on His shoulders, and save it not only by calling it back, but also by carrying it along. Let the Lord seek His image, wash away from it all accumulated uncleanness that has stained it and so brighten up the mirror of the human heart. For it is written: *Who can make clean that is conceived of unclean seed? Is it not Thou who only art?*[84] Let the Lord seek His image that in its renovation and justification the grace of its Reformer may appear, as the Apostle Paul testifies to have happened to himself when he says: *And I was unknown by face to the churches of Judea, which were in Christ. . . . They had heard only that he*

*who persecuted us in times past doth now preach the faith
which ... he impugned. And they glorified God in me.*[85]
Such was the conviction of the Christian people at that
time, such the belief of the first members of the Church
who had but one heart and one soul: [86] when they saw a
man converted from his error to the acceptance of the
truth, they gave glory to God and confessed that the
convert's faith came from a divine gift.[87] The Lord Himself when instructing His disciples, the teachers of all
nations, said: *So let your light shine before men, that,
seeing your good works, they may magnify your Father
who is in heaven.*[88]

## CHAPTER 9

*When Scripture speaks of the good or the wicked, of the
elect or the reprobate, it mentions one class of men in
such wise that it seems as though no one is omitted.*

It is in our own best interest, therefore, to hold that
all good things, especially those conducive to eternal life,
are obtained through God's favour, increased through
God's favour, and preserved through God's favour.[89] With
this faith firmly fixed and rooted in our hearts, I think
our religious sense ought not to be disturbed by the problem of the total or only partial conversion of mankind.
This is a condition we must keep—that we do not permit
what is inaccessible to our knowledge to render obscure
what we know clearly, and that we do not, whilst wantonly
insisting on knowing what we cannot know, lose sight of

what we are able to know; [90] since it ought to be enough
for us to live on with the knowledge that we have gained.[91]

[For, this we do know beyond any doubt: all beginning
and all increase of merit is for every man a gift of God.
Moreover, it is impossible that He who wills all men to be
saved would, for no reasons whatever, not save the greater
part of them. But we are not able to know these reasons,
which would not have remained secret had it been necessary for us to know them. Here our faith is to be tested
in the things that are not visible; and we have always to
preserve our reverence for God's justice even when we do
not understand its course.][92]

What wonder, indeed, if some men do not come to the
sacraments of life [93] when they who seemed to have come
to them fall away? Of such it is said: *They went out
from us, but they were not of us. For if they had been
of us, they would no doubt have remained with us.*[94] Like
unto these are they who *profess that they know God, but
in their works . . . deny Him.*[95] For, though it be written,
*Whosoever shall call upon the name of the Lord, shall be
saved,*[96] yet of some the Lord says: *Not every one that
saith to me, Lord, Lord, shall enter into the kingdom of
heaven; but he that doth the will of my Father who is in
heaven, he shall enter into the kingdom of heaven;* [97] and,
*Many will say to me in that day: Lord, Lord, have we not
prophesied in Thy name and cast out devils in Thy name
and done many miracles in Thy name? And then will I
say unto them: I never knew you. Depart from me, you
workers of iniquity.*[98] Such people do not really invoke
the name of the Lord because they do not have *the Spirit
of adoption of sons, whereby we cry: Abba (Father).*[99]
But, *No man can say The Lord Jesus, but by the Holy*

*Spirit;* [100] and, *Whosoever are led by the Spirit of God, they are the sons of God.* [101]

They who come to God through God and with the desire of being saved, are saved without fail, for they conceive the very desire of salvation through God's inspiration, and thanks to an illumination from Him who calls, they come to the knowledge of the truth. They are indeed the sons of promise, the reward of faith, the spiritual progeny of Abraham, *a chosen generation, a kingly priesthood,* [102] foreknown and foreordained [103] for eternal life according to the testimony of the Holy Spirit expressed by the prophet Jeremias: *Behold the days shall come, saith the Lord, and I will make a new covenant with the house of Israel and with the house of Juda; not according to the covenant which I made with their fathers, in the day that I took them by the hand to bring them out of the land of Egypt, for they did not persevere in my covenant, and I left them aside, saith the Lord. This is the covenant that I will make with the house of Israel after those days, saith the Lord: I will give my laws in their understanding, and I will write them in their hearts; and I will be their God, and they shall be my people. And no man shall teach his neighbour, and no man his brother, saying: Know the Lord. For all shall know me from the small among them even to the great . . . , for I will forgive their iniquities and I will remember their sins no more.* [104] *And I will give them another way and another heart that they may fear me all days for their good and that of their children after them. And I will make an everlasting covenant with them which I will not take away from them; and I will give my fear in their heart, that they*

*may not revolt from me, and I will visit them, that I may
make them good.*[105]

Through Isaias also the Lord foretells the same things
about His grace by which He fashions all men into a new
creation. He says: *Behold, I do new things which shall
spring forth, and you shall know them; I will make a
way in the wilderness and rivers in the dry land. The
beasts of the field shall bless me, the sirens and the young
of ostriches, because I have given water in the wilderness
and rivers in the dry land, to give drink to my chosen
race, to my people whom I have won unto me that they
may preach my powers.*[106] And again: *I have sworn by
myself, justice alone shall go out of my mouth and my
words shall not be turned away; for every knee shall be
bowed to me, and every tongue shall confess to God.*[107]

If, then, it is not possible that these things shall not
take place, because God's foreknowledge is not faltering
and His design not changeable, nor His will inefficacious
nor His promise false,[108] then all, without any exception,
about whom these predictions were made are saved. He
establishes His laws in their understanding and writes
them with His finger in their hearts, so that they recognize
God not through the working of human learning, but
through the teaching of the Supreme Instructor;[109] for
*neither he that planteth is anything, nor he that water-
eth, but God that giveth the increase.*[110] All these, *from
the small to the great, know God,*[111] because they have
heard and learned from the Father how to come to Christ.
All of them, led out of error, are directed towards the way
of life. To all is it given, with a change of heart, to know
the right thing and to will it. In all is implanted the fear
that makes them keep [112] the commandments of God. A

road is opened in the desert, the parched land is watered with streams. They who formerly did not open their mouths to praise God but like dumb and irrational animals had taken on the ferocity of beasts,[113] now, having drunk[114] at the fountain of the divine pronouncements, bless and praise God and recount the power and wonders of His mercy, how He chose them and adopted them to be His sons and made them heirs of the New Testament. Now if, as the Apostle says, *a man's testament, if it be confirmed, no man despiseth nor addeth to it,*[115] how, then, could a divine promise in any manner be possibly made void?

What, then, the Lord promised to Abraham without a condition and gave without a law, remains absolutely firm and sees its fulfilment every day.[116] It is true, some who have heard this preached to them have not believed, yet *their unbelief has not made the faith of God without effect. For God is true and every man a liar.*[117] Obviously, men who have heard the Gospel and refused to believe, are all the more inexcusable than if they had not listened to any preaching of the truth. But it is certain that in God's foreknowledge they were not sons of Abraham and were not reckoned among the number of them of whom it is said, *In thy seed all the tribes of the earth shall be blessed.*[118] He promised them the faith when He said: *And no man shall teach his neighbour, and no man his brother, saying: Know the Lord. For all shall know me from the small among them even to the great.*[119] He promised them pardon when He said, *I will forgive their iniquities and I will remember their sins no more.*[120] He promised them an obedient heart when He said, *I will give them another heart and another way, that they may fear me all days.*[121] He promised them perseverance when He said, *I will give my fear in their heart, that they may not revolt from me, and I will visit them, that I may make them good.*[122] Finally, to all without exception He promised the faith [123] when He said: *I have sworn by myself, justice alone shall go out of my mouth, and my words shall not be turned away; for every knee shall be bowed to me, and every tongue shall confess to God.*[124]

If, then, we were to say that what God has sworn to do will not take place, we would be ascribing—heaven forbid!—falsehood to God and a lie to Truth. Our religious faith prompts us to say that God's words do not fail, that what He has decreed must come to pass. How, then, are we to be convinced of the absolute truth of His promise, when many thousands of men still serve demons and bow their knees before idols? [125] Only by remembering this: such pronouncements of God are made according to that unchangeable knowledge [126] in which He sees all mankind already divided. Whether He speaks of the good only or of the wicked only, He does so in such a manner that He seems to omit no one.[127] Thus, when the Apostle says: *The old things are passed away. Behold, all things are made new,*[128] does he not seem to say that *all* men have been renewed? Or when he says: *Because in Him it hath well pleased the Father that all fulness should dwell, and through Him to reconcile all things unto Himself,*[129] does he not speak as if he meant us to understand that *no one* is excluded from this reconciliation? Or when he says: (God) *in these latter days hath spoken to us by His Son, whom He hath appointed heir of all things,*[130] does the statement as it stands mean anything else than that all men have been transferred by the

Father into Christ's inheritance, according to the prophecy of David who said: *Ask of me, and I will give Thee the Gentiles for Thy inheritance, and the utmost parts of the earth for Thy possession?* [131] And when the Lord says, *If I be lifted up from the earth, I will draw all things to myself,* [132] does it not look as if He promised the conversion of each and every one? Or when a prophecy about the Church says: *Every valley shall be filled and every mountain and hill shall be made low; and the crooked shall become straight, and the rough ways plain,* [133] would one think that any man is passed by, any man not indicated as a future subject of Christ? And what about this text, *And all flesh shall come before my face, to adore in Jerusalem, saith the Lord;* [134] or this one, *And it shall come to pass in those days, that I will pour out my Spirit upon all flesh;* [135] and this one, *The Lord lifteth up all that fall; and setteth up all that are cast down?* [136] Does it not sound as if no one is excluded from this favour of God?

God's people, therefore, has a completeness all its own. It is true that a great part of mankind refuse or neglect the grace of their Saviour. In the elect, however, and the foreknown who were set apart from the generality of mankind, we have a specified totality. [137] Thus the whole world is spoken of as though the whole of it had been liberated, and all mankind as though all men had been chosen. [138] So, too, in the texts concerning the reprobate the divine Author speaks in such a way that what He says of a certain part of mankind He seems to say of the whole of it. [139] A case in point is this word of John the Baptist: *He that cometh from heaven is above all. And what He hath seen and heard, that He testifieth; and no man receiveth His testimony.*[140] Or this saying of the Apostle, *All seek the things that are their own, not the things that are Jesus Christ's.*[141] Or these versicles of the Davidian psalm: *The Lord hath looked down from heaven upon the children of men, to see if there be any that understand and seek God. They are all gone aside, they are become unprofitable together; there is none that doth good, not one.*[142]

From these and other texts which could easily be multiplied by anyone looking for them, it is shown beyond doubt that the whole earth is at times mentioned for a part of it, the whole world for a part of the world and all mankind for a section of it.[143] In these texts, however, Scripture itself is generally quick to indicate the necessary restriction, drawing the reader's attention away from the whole that is expressly stated, to the part that is to be understood by it.[144] Take, for example, this word of the Apostle: *We preach Christ crucified: unto the Jews indeed a stumbling block and unto the Gentiles foolishness; but unto them that are called, both Jews and Greeks, Christ, the power of God and the wisdom of God.*[145] Is Christ actually a power for those to whom He is a stumbling block? Again, is He both wisdom and foolishness to some? No—some of these will be justified through faith whilst others will become hardened in irreligion. Thus, in one group, including both believers and unbelievers, he sets apart some, namely *the called.*[146] In that way, he pointed out, those whom he had said to be alien to the faith, are also excluded from the call, though they had heard the Gospel.[147]

## CHAPTER 10

*Scripture speaks of the elect and the reprobate in one nation as though it meant the same persons.*[148]

According to the same rule,[149] Sacred Scripture makes a promise through Isaias: *I will lead the blind into the way they know not; and in the paths which they are ignorant of they will walk. I will make darkness light before them, and crooked things straight. These things shall I do, and I shall not forsake them.*[150] But what follows, *They are turned back,*[151] is to be applied to one part of their race, not to those of whom it is said, *I shall not forsake them.* Again the Lord says to Jacob: *Fear not, for I am with thee. I will bring thy seed from the east, and gather thee from the west. I will say to the north: Bring them; and to the south: Keep them not back. Bring my sons from afar and my daughters from the ends of the earth, all those among whom my name is called upon. I have created him for my glory, I have fashioned him and made him.*[152] But what follows, *And I brought forth a blind people, and their eyes are blind, and they have deaf ears,*[153] can in no way apply to those whom He says He has prepared for His glory. In fact, of all these sayings uttered about one race of men a first set applies to some persons, a second to others.

In the Apostle also we find narrated under the name of the whole people what concerns only a part of them, and this remaining part[154] is reckoned as a totality. For instance, discoursing about the blindness of the Jews and at the same time showing that some of them were saved through grace, he says: *I say then: Hath God cast away*

*His people? God forbid! For I also am an Israelite of the seed of Abraham, of the tribe of Benjamin. God hath not cast away His people which He foreknew.*[155]

So, this foreknown people, this people not cast away, these are the justified in Christ. What seems to be affirmed of all Israel is shown to apply to those only whom grace chose for its own,[156] as the sequel of the Apostle's discourse relates. He goes on to say: *Know you not what the Scripture saith of Elias, how he calleth on God against Israel? "Lord, they have slain Thy prophets, they have dug down Thy altars. And I am left alone, and they seek my life." But what saith the divine answer to him? "I have left me seven thousand men that have not bowed their knees to Baal." Even so then,*[157] *at this present time also there is a remnant saved according to the election of grace. And if by grace, it is not now by works; otherwise grace is no more grace.*[158] Not the whole of Israel, therefore, was rejected; nor was the whole of it chosen. Rather, a wilful blindness turned away one section, while the light of grace kept the other as its own.[159] And yet they are spoken of as if no division had been made of the whole people, in those who perish and those who are saved. For when we read: *As concerning the Gospel, indeed, they are enemies for your sake; but as touching the election of God, they are beloved for the sake of the fathers,*[160] it sounds as though he called "beloved" those whom he has termed "enemies." But the Apostle himself dispelled this obscurity by adding *that blindness in part has happened in Israel.*[161] We have to understand that one genus is divided into two species and that expressions like "all men," "all fulness," "all Israel," need not always designate a totality but often only a part.[162]

## CHAPTER 11

*Scripture speaks of men of different ages as if
they were one and the same generation.*

Among these various ways of speaking found in Scripture there is still another to which we should turn our
attention. What refers to men of different ages is presented as if it applied to but one generation, to men of
one lifetime.[163] Thus the Apostle Saint Peter, writing for
the people of his own time and of the future, says: *But
you are a chosen generation, a kingly priesthood, a holy
nation, a purchased people; that you may declare His
virtues, who hath called you out of darkness into His
marvellous light; who in time past were not a people,
but now are the people of God; who had not obtained
mercy, but now have obtained mercy.*[164] Were, at the time
of this preaching, all those men still alive whom God *in
times past suffered to walk in their own ways?*[165] And
those who had once been delivered unto their own desires,
are they identically the same people who now will be
*called*[166] *out of the darkness into His marvellous light?*
Had they not already died in their ignorance? Were
they any longer in the world? And was there any return
from error to truth for those who had died in times past?
Yet in speaking, usage is such that when grace conquered
the descendants of the ungodly, we seem to say[167] that
those are chosen now who were once forsaken. What is
said here, however, does not apply to the same men but to
men of the same race. The call which appeared at the
approach of the end of the world[168] has no retrospective

effect on the past ages. So those about whom these things are successively said are, in a sense, the same men and yet not the same men. While in one case special considerations are not distinguished from general ones, in another they are.[169]

CHAPTER 12

*The word of the Apostle, "who will have all men to be saved," is to be understood in its entire and full meaning.*

When devotees of sophistical wranglings [170] read or hear this, they will object that our arguments contradict and fulness, we mean to take nothing from the context the Apostle who teaches that *God will have all men to be saved and to come to the knowledge of the truth.*[171] We accept this brief sentence of the Apostle in its entirety preceding it or following it.[172] Let us leave aside all other testimonies of the inspired writings. This one passage will do to refute their slanderous objection and to defend what they impiously deny.

Now, then, the Apostle Paul, teacher of the Gentiles, writing to Timothy, says: *I desire, therefore, first of all, that supplications, intercessions, thanksgivings be made for all men, for kings and for all that are in high station: that we may lead a quiet and peaceable life in all piety and chastity. For this is good and acceptable in the sight of God our Saviour, who will have all men to be saved and to come to the knowledge of the truth. For there is one God and one Mediator of God and men, the man Christ Jesus who gave Himself a redemption for all.* [173] For the universal Church this constitutes a fundamental norm of the Apostle's teaching.[174] Let us, then, seek the mind of the universal Church about it in order not to understand it amiss by relying on our own judgment. There can be no doubt about what is enjoined, if the efforts made by all those who obey are the same.[175]

The Apostle commands—rather, the Lord speaking through the Apostle commands through him—*that suppli-cations and intercessions, thanksgivings be made for all men, for kings and for all that are in high station.*[176] All priests and all the faithful adhere unanimously to this norm of supplication in their devotions. There is no part of the world in which Christian peoples do not offer up these prayers. The Church, then, pleads before God everywhere, not only for the saints [177] and those regen-erated in Christ, but also for all infidels and all enemies of the Cross of Christ, for all worshippers of idols, for all who persecute Christ in His members, for the Jews whose blindness does not see the light of the gospel, for heretics and schismatics who are alien to the unity of faith and charity.[178]

But what does she beg for them if not that they leave their errors and be converted to God, that they accept the faith, accept charity, that they be freed from the shadows of ignorance and come to the knowledge of the truth? They cannot do this by themselves: they are struggling under the weight of vicious habits and are ensnared by the bonds of Satan. They are powerless before their own deceptions; so stubbornly do they cling to them that they love falsehood in the measure truth should be loved. Hence the merciful and just Lord wishes that prayers be offered Him for all men. When we see countless souls drawn out of such deep misery, we should have no doubt that God is granting a prayerful request. While thanking Him for those who are saved, we should hopefully pray that the same divine grace may deliver from the power of darkness those who are still without light and conduct them into the kingdom of God before they depart this life.[179]

## CHAPTER 13

*We cannot understand in this life the deep mystery, why the grace of God passes by some men for whom the Church offers prayers.*

We indeed see it happen that the grace of the Saviour passes by some men and that the prayers of the Church in their favour are not heard.[180] This must be ascribed to the secret judgments of divine justice. We must acknowledge that we cannot understand this profound mystery in this life.[181] *For we know in part, and we prophesy in part;* [182] and *we see now through a glass in a dark manner.*[183] We are neither wiser nor better informed than the most blessed Apostle. When he entered into the secret of these great mysteries in explaining the power of grace, he was overcome by the things that are beyond all utterance. He said: *For I would not have you ignorant, brethren, of this mystery (lest you should be wise in your own conceits) that blindness in part has happened in Israel, until the fulness of the Gentiles should come in. And so all Israel should be saved, as it is written: "There shall come out of Sion, He that shall deliver and shall turn away ungodliness from Jacob. And this is to them my covenant: when I shall take away their sins."* [184]

*As concerning the gospel, indeed, they are enemies for your sake; but as touching the election, they are most dear for the sake of the fathers. For the gifts and the calling of God are without repentance. For as you also in times past did not believe God, but now have obtained mercy, through their unbelief: so these also now have not believed, for your mercy, that they also may obtain mercy. For God hath concluded all in unbelief, that He may have mercy on all.*[185]

Enraptured, as it were, he had poured out these mysterious statements on the divine ways which are beyond all bounds of human understanding; then, as though dazed, he broke off all logical sequence in his discourse.[186] Astounded at the things he had uttered, he exclaimed: *O the depth of the riches of the wisdom and of the knowledge of God! How incomprehensible are His judgments, and how unsearchable His ways! For who hath known the mind of the Lord? Or who hath been His counsellor? Or who hath first given to Him, and recompense shall be made him? For of Him, and by Him, and in Him, are all things: to Him be glory for ever. Amen.*[187]

Quite obviously, what he had been teaching above, raised many questions.[188] For example, one could inquire why God's grace works in a different way in many peoples and ages. Why, namely, were all nations in former ages left to walk in their own ways,[189] when Israel alone was singled out to be instructed by God's own words and was chosen to know the truth, whereas in the end her unbelief was to be the occasion for the salvation of the Gentiles? Could not the mercy of God, because this one people persevered in its ancestral faith, bestow itself also on the other nations? Indeed, why could not they whose downfall means salvation for the nations, be freed from their blindness before *the fulness of the Gentiles should come in?* [190] Could they not receive the light at one time with all mankind, they, who after the conversion of all nations will yet be saved? Or how [191] can the whole of Israel be freed from its blindness and saved when a countless number of them die in unbelief and never obtain the promised chance for salvation? Or how can one say of the Gentiles, too, who were not called at first, that the fulness of them now comes in, when so many thousands of men of every age and station in life, in all the nations that live under the sun, die without the justification of Christ? But the reasons of these mysterious decrees our God-fearing and learned teacher preferred to leave hidden in the depth of the riches of the wisdom and knowledge of God, rather than rashly to seek what is withheld from our human knowledge, namely, the secret of the most just Truth and the most merciful Goodness. He omitted nothing of what we should know, but he did not touch on what is not given to us to see. [192]

## CHAPTER 14

*In the dispensation of God's works the reasons of many things remain hidden and only the facts are manifest.*

In the divine economy the reasons of many things actually remain hidden and only the facts become known. [193] We see what takes place, we do not see why it happens. The event itself is plain, its reason is kept hidden. Thus about the same event no one can presume to scrutinize the inscrutable or to deny falsely what is evident. I do not know, for example, why this man was created a Greek and that one a barbarian, why this one was born in wealth and another in destitution; why the strength and beauty of a stately body exalts this one, whilst the withered thinness of feeble limbs deforms that man; why one is born of Catholic stock and nourished in the cradle of the faith, while another is a child of heretics and drinks with his mother's milk the poison of error.

A thousand other differences in the conditions of the bodies and the qualities of the minds, in the circumstances of time and the customs of the countries, I cannot account for. But I do not for that reason fail to know that God is the Creator and Ruler of all these things. He did indeed create the bodies and souls of each and every man. Besides the diversity following from the pursuits which each man chooses, He himself produces a great and manifold diversity at the very beginning of each one's existence.[194] Braggarts with their many fancies would disturb us and lead us astray: they rashly presumed to explain the unknown and ascribe these original inequalities to the fates [195]— which do not exist—or to the stars.[196] But we know with absolute certitude that God our Creator forms each individual from the original elements just as He pleases, and that though bodies are of one nature and souls of one nature, He tempers them according to the measures most agreeable to Him.[197] These works of God would not be withdrawn from our human understanding, were there any need for us to know them. It would be revealed *why* each particular event takes place, were it not sufficient to know *that* it happens.[198]

The Lord says to Moses, *Who gave man a mouth, or who made dumb and deaf, seeing and blind? Did not I, the Lord God?* [199] And through Isaias, *Behold, is it not I who made barren and fecund? saith the Lord.* [200] The Book of Ecclesiasticus reads, *Good things and evil, life and death, poverty and riches, are from God.* [201] And Job says, *The tabernacles of robbers abound, and they provoke God boldly; whereas it is He that hath given all into their hands.* [202] The same, treating about the growth and decline of all human things and ascribing all changes to God's judgments, says again: *With Him is wisdom and strength, He hath counsel and understanding. If He pull down, there is no man that can build up. If He shut up a man, there is none that can open. If He withhold the waters, all things shall be dried up; if He send them out, they shall overturn the earth. With Him is strength and wisdom; He knoweth both the deceiver and him that is deceived. He bringeth counsellors to a foolish end, and judges to insensibility. He looseth the belt of kings, and girdeth their loins with a cord. He leadeth away priests without glory, and overthroweth nobles. He changeth the speech of the true speakers, and taketh away the doctrine of the aged. He poureth contempt upon princes, and relieveth them that were oppressed. He discovereth deep things out of darkness, and bringeth up to light the shadow of death. He multiplieth nations and destroyeth them, and will restore them again after they were overthrown. He changeth the heart of the princes of the earth and deceiveth them, that they walk in vain where there is no way. They shall grope as in the dark, and not in the light; and He shall make them stagger like men that are drunk.* [203] And again, explaining that God's will can-

not be frustrated, he says, *For He is alone, and no man
can turn away His thought. And whatsoever His soul
desireth, that will He do.*[204]

### CHAPTER 15

*We may not attribute the salvation of a part of mankind
to their own merits, as if grace chose the
good and passed by the wicked.*[205]

One section of mankind attains salvation, the other
perishes. Were we to ascribe this to individual merits and
say that grace left off the wicked and chose the good, then
we would be faced with the case of countless peoples to
whom for so many ages no messenger of the heavenly
doctrine has appeared.[206] And we should not say that their
posterity were better than they, for it is written of them:
*The nation of the Gentiles that was sitting in darkness
has seen a great light; and to them that were sitting in
darkness and the shadow of death, light is risen;* [207] and it
is to these that the Apostle Peter says: *But you are a chosen
generation, a kingly priesthood, a holy nation, a purchased
people, that you may declare His virtues, who hath called
you out of darkness into His marvellous light; who in time
past were not a people, but are now the people of God; on
whom once He had no mercy, but now He shows mercy.*[208]
Therefore, what the fathers [209] did not merit, the sons did
not receive on account of their merits. For indeed, fathers
and sons alike were steeped in irreligion, the blindness of
ignorance plunged them both in the same errors.

But who is so learned as to understand, or who is so wise as to discover why God did not have mercy on the former, but was merciful towards the latter? The reason of this discrimination escapes us; the difference itself we see. We do not understand God's judgment, but we see His work. Shall we accuse His justice which is hidden, when we must give thanks for His mercy which is manifest? No, let us praise and reverence God's action, while there is no risk in not knowing what He keeps veiled.[210]

### CHAPTER 16

*Before the use of reason all children are alike, yet some*
*pass to eternal life, others to eternal death; this*
*is a proof of God's inscrutable judgments.*

Consider also [211] the case of the whole multitude of children. In none of them do you find deserts, neither past nor future, only the sin in which the whole human race is born unto damnation. We speak now of children before the use of reason and before they are able to make any use of their free will. Some are regenerated in baptism and pass on to eternal happiness, others are not reborn and go to unending misery.[212]

You may say, they have original sin; yes, they have it, but all are equally guilty. Or you look for moral innocence; agreed, but none of them has sinned. Our human sense of justice can see no reason for discrimination, but God's ineffable grace finds subjects for election.[213] His design is secret, but His gift is manifest. It is His mercy that inspires the work, His power that hides from us the reason. But both what we see and what we do not see is equally above suspicion. When He is the Author of what we see taking place, we cannot withhold our praise of His justice, though it surpasses our understanding.[214]

## CHAPTER 17

*Deathbed conversions of sinners are a proof that grace is given unmerited and that God's judgments are inscrutable.*

Now turn your attention to the case of sinners who after a long lifetime of shame and crime receive new life in the sacrament of Christ's baptism just before they depart from this world.[215] Without any good works to plead for them they are admitted to the communion of the kingdom of heaven. How will you understand this judgment of God? You can only confess unhesitatingly that God's gifts are unmerited. There are no crimes so hateful that can prevent the gift of grace, just as there can be no good works so excellent that can claim as their just reward what God gives gratuitously.[216]

Suppose that justification, which is the work of grace, were due to previous merits; suppose it were like the pay of a labourer rather than the gift of a Donor: would not then our Redemption in the blood of Christ be debased, and the initiative claimed by human works refuse to yield to God's mercy? [217] And how could you then show that no human industry is able to remove original sin? You could never show it unless both unbelievers and sinners were through the laver of Christ admitted into His kingdom; and unless they who glory in their innocence acknowledge how they can really do nothing worthy of the adoption of the sons of God when they have not received the sacrament of regeneration. For in this respect they are in the same condition as the greatest sinners; regenerated in baptism they are alike in sanctity; take away baptism, and they perish all together.[218]

It is a fact, then, that grace seeks its adopted sons even among the worst sinners in their very last moments, and that many who looked less wicked are denied this gift. But who could say that these facts escape God's ruling or that He decrees them without a profound justice? [219] And, obviously, there is no injustice here merely because this is shrouded in mystery, rather there is justice because it flows from God's decree. In fact, for what depends solely on God's free decision we cannot know definitely what His judgment will be, before He decrees the facts.[220] But when the facts have taken place, no one is left free to complain of the outcome of God's decree, for it is altogether certain that He had not to act otherwise than He did.[221]

He Himself has illustrated the diversity of His manifold calling, pertaining to the same grace, by the celebrated example of the Gospel parable. There He shows a householder who hires workmen for his vineyard at different hours of the day on a contract of a denarius a day.[222] Now, it is clear that the man sent to the vineyard at the eleventh hour to work with those who had laboured the whole day, represents the class of people of whom we are now treating. God's mercy shows them this generosity at the decline of the day, that is, at the end of their life, to reveal the excellence of His grace. For He does not pay the price

of their labour, but showers on them whom He has chosen
without works of their own, the riches of His goodness.
Thus they also who laboured the whole day long in the
sweat of their brow and did not receive more than the
latecomers, have to understand that they were given a
gratuitous gift, not the reward of their labours.

Shall we, too, murmur against the Householder because He gives the same wages to those called last and to
the full-time labourers, and because no greater compen-
sation is earned by much labour than by labour that is
scarcely existent? Then we shall have to hear what one
of those men was told: *Friend, I do thee no wrong. Didst
thou not agree with me for a penny? Take what is thine
and go thy way. I will also give to this last even as to thee.
Or, is it not lawful for me to do with my property what
I will? Or, is thy eye evil because I am good?* [223] Clearly,
to this grumbler such liberality seemed unjust.[224] What
lesson was he taught? What explanation was he given?
He was not told anything as to the justice of this ruling;
he was not given any insight into the hidden mystery. But
that he might refrain from discussing God's judgments,
he was confronted with the goodness of His mercy and
the power of His will.[225] The Apostle's word might have
been addressed to Him also: *O man, who art thou that
repliest against God? Shall the thing formed say to Him
that formed it: Why hast Thou made me thus?* [226]

CHAPTER 18

*Grace, the condition sine qua non of all merit, is given
unmerited purely out of God's good pleasure.*

God's will, therefore, is the sole reason why grace is
bestowed on any man, whatever be his nation or race, his
state or age.[227] In that will does the motive of his election
lie hidden. Merit begins with grace, which was itself
received unmerited. If merit could be gained without
grace, we would not have these words, *Unless a man be
born again of water and the Holy Spirit, he cannot enter
into the kingdom of God;*[228] and, *Except you eat the flesh
of the Son of man and drink His blood, you shall not have
life in you;*[229] we would rather hear, "Unless a man be
just and good he cannot attain eternal happiness."

There would be no need of being born again of water
and of the Spirit, if it were sufficient to know the Law.[230]
We believe that in baptism all sins are forgiven; this faith
would be vain if we were taught that grace is not given
to the wicked and the ungodly, but only to the good and
the righteous. Thus the source of true life and of true
justice lies in the sacrament of regeneration. When man
is born again, then his virtues begin to be true,[231] then
they[232] who could hardly gain an earthly reward of vain
praise,[233] begin through faith to advance towards eternal
glory. Before a man is justified, be he a Jew proud of his
knowledge of the Law or a Greek conceited with the study
of natural wisdom, he is imprisoned under sin.[234] Were
he to persist in his unbelief, the anger of God would remain upon him, the anger incurred in Adam's sin.

The Apostle speaks of this where he says: *And you, when you were dead in your offences and sins, wherein in times past you walked according to the course of this world, according to the prince of the power of this air, of the spirit that now worketh on the children of unbelief; in which also we conversed in time past, in the desires of our flesh, fulfilling the will of the flesh and of our thoughts, and were by nature children of wrath, even as the rest;* [235] and again: *That you were at that time without Christ, being aliens from the conversation of Israel and strangers to the testament, having no hope of the promise and without God in the world;* [236] and again: *You were heretofore darkness, but now light in the Lord;* [237] and again: *Giving thanks to God the Father, who hath made us worthy to be partakers of the lot of the saints in light; who hath delivered us from darkness and the power of darkness and hath translated us into the kingdom of the Son of His love;* [238] and again: *For we ourselves also were some time unwise, incredulous, erring, slaves of divers desires and pleasures, living in malice and envy, hateful and hating one another. But when the goodness and kindness of our Saviour appeared, not by the works of justice which we have done, but according to His mercy, He saved us by the laver of regeneration of the Holy Spirit. Whom He hath poured forth upon us abundantly, through Jesus Christ our Saviour: that being justified by His grace, we may be heirs according to the hope of life everlasting.*[239]

## CHAPTER 19

*What nature is without grace.*

To explain in a very few words what human nature is without grace,[240] let the Apostle Jude tell us what both the ignorance of the uncultured and the learning of the wise produce. *But these men,* he says, *blaspheme whatever things they know not; and what things soever they naturally know, like dumb beasts, in these they are corrupted.*[241] Let also the Evangelist Luke tell us in the words of Zacharias what night envelops the human race before the light of grace shines on it, and from what shadows of ignorance God's people is freed. *And thou, child,* he says, *shalt be called the prophet of the Highest; for thou shalt go before the face of the Lord to prepare His ways, to give knowledge of salvation to His people unto the remission of their sins, on account of the bowels of the mercy of the Lord, in which the Orient from on high hath visited us, to shine before them that sit in darkness and in the shadow of death; to direct our feet into the way of peace.*[242]

## CHAPTER 20

*Our Lord in His deep mercy wishes to save all nations and is actually working for their salvation, yet it is true that no one accepts His word.*

In this His deep mercy, the Lord wishes not only to redeem one people but to save all nations,[243] as the Evangelist says: *That Jesus should die for the nation. And not only for the nation, but also to gather together in one the dispersed children of God.*[244] That is the meaning of our Lord's great proclamation which, like a trumpet resounding with His loving-kindness throughout the world, invites and summons all men. For after He had said: *I confess to Thee, O Father, Lord of heaven and earth, because Thou hast hid these things from the wise and the prudent and hast revealed them to the little ones. Yea, Father; for so hath it seemed good in Thy sight,* He added: *All things are delivered to me by my Father. And no one knoweth the Son, but the Father: neither doth any one know the Father, but the Son and he to whom it shall please the Son to reveal Him;* and then further: *Come to me, all you that labour and are burdened, and I will refresh you. Take up my yoke upon you and learn of me, because I am meek and humble of heart; and you shall find rest to your souls. For my yoke is sweet and my burden light.*[245] John the Baptist, too, proclaims with prophetic insight, in the Gospel of John: *He that cometh from heaven is above all. What He hath seen and heard, He testifieth; and no man receiveth His testimony. He that receiveth His testimony, hath set to his seal that God is true.*[246]

Reflecting, therefore, the blindness which the human race contracted in its long night of ignorance and pride, the Creator of the world came into the world, *and the world knew Him not;*[247] *The light shineth in darkness, and the darkness did not comprehend it;*[248] *He . . . is above all; what He hath seen and heard, that He testifieth; and no man receiveth His testimony.*[249] But not in vain did God, the Son of God, come into this world and give Himself for all and die, *not only for the nation, but to gather in one* the dispersed children of God.[250] And He says to all, *Come to me, all you that labour and are burdened.*[251] Keeping to Himself the deciding motive of an election that is unknowable to us, He communicates the knowledge of Himself and of the Father to whomsoever He chooses to reveal it.[252]

For these reasons do all the sons of light, sons of the promise, sons of Abraham, sons of God, a chosen people, a kingly priesthood, true Israelites, foreknown and foreordained for the kingdom of God who has called them not only from among the Jews but also from among the Gentiles,[253] accept the word of Him who came down from heaven, and by so doing, they seal God's truthfulness; that is, they clearly show in their own salvation that God is truthful, namely, that He is actually fulfilling the promise He made to Abraham, the father of all the nations. When he was promised by God that he was to be the heir of the world, he *staggered not by distrust; but was strengthened in faith, giving glory to God and most fully knowing that what He has promised, He is able also to perform.*[254] But who is so alien to Abraham's faith, who has sunk so low in his descent from the father of all nations as to say that God's promise is not fulfilled or that it is fulfilled by another than Him who made it? That man would be a liar. But God is truthful, and everyone who accepts His word is a living witness proclaiming that God's light shining on him made him see, made him obey, made him understand. This John the Evangelist attests, saying: *We know that . . . the whole world is seated in wickedness. And we know that the Son of God is come. And He hath given us understanding that we may know the true God and may be in His true Son.*[255]

CHAPTER 21

*We must not seek to know why God chooses some*
*and not others, nor why in the past He left aside*
*all the Gentiles and chose Israel alone.*

You may ask why the Saviour of all men did not give
to all the understanding which enables men to know the
true God, and to be, that is, to remain, *in His true Son.*[256]
Although we believe that the help of grace was never fully
withheld from any one (we shall treat of this more fully
in the following [257]), yet the reason you ask about remains
veiled in much the same way as is hidden from us the motive for which God formerly left aside all the Gentiles and
took one people for His own in order to raise them to the
knowledge of the truth. If we must not complain of this
latter judgment of God, much less can we murmur against
His way of ruling the election of all the Gentiles. We must
not scrutinize what God wants to be hidden, but we may
not disregard what He made manifest, else we may be
wrongly inquisitive about the former and deserve blame
for not gratefully receiving the latter.[258]

We know quite well that some people [259] are so incon-
siderate in their presumption and so arrogant in their
pride that they dare to profane with their pretended learning what the great Teacher of the Gentiles was taught *not*
*of men, neither by men,*[260] but by God, and what he confessed to be far above all limitations of his knowledge.
They would see nothing mysterious or secret in those
things of which the Apostle refrained from giving any

explanation, and only made plain what we must not search into. As we have already said above,[261] it is not given to any human study or genius to explore the decree and design according to which God, who is invariably good, invariably just, ever foreknowing, ever omnipotent, *hath concluded all in unbelief, that He may have mercy on all;* [262] yet He delayed for centuries, while He was educating Israel, to enlighten the countless peoples of infidels; and now He allows that same Israel to go blind till the universality of the Gentiles enter the fold. He allows so many thousands of this people to be born and die to be lost, when only those whom the end of the world will find alive will attain salvation.[263] From the explanation which all the Scriptures give of this mystery we learn what has happened in the past, what is taking place at present, and what remains to come about. But why God's good pleasure decreed all this, is withheld from the ken of human understanding.

CHAPTER 22

*Those who see in human merit the reason why God distinquishes between some whom He selects and others whom He does not elect, teach that no one is saved gratuitously but only in justice; the case of infants refutes their position.*

Those men who feel ashamed to acknowledge ignorance in any matter, and who when faced with an obscure question throw out their snares of deception,[264] see in human merit the reason why God discerns whom He has elected [265] and whom He has not—for *many are called but few are chosen.*[266] Consequently, they teach that no one is saved gratuitously but only in justice, because all men are able by natural means to discover the truth if they wish, and grace is given freely to all who beg for it.[267]

This statement,[268] not to speak now of what is really meant by grace,[269] may be able to show some sort of pretence in the case of adults who have the use of their free will. But for infants who lack altogether the merit of a will to do good and who, just like all other mortals, are wounded with original sin, they can offer no explanation whatever. Why are some of them regenerated in baptism and saved, while others fail to be reborn and are lost? [270] How can this happen in spite of the Providence and omnipotence of Him *in whose hand is the soul of every living thing and the spirit of all flesh of man,*[271] and to whom was said, *The days of man are short, and the number of his days is with Thee?* [272]

But I do not think that these patrons of human liberty will so impudently misuse the simplicity of men as to assert that all this happens by chance, or that the unbaptised are not lost.[273] For then they would show plainly that they either share the views of the pagans about fate, or deny with the Pelagians that Adam's sin is transmitted to his posterity. But even the Pelagians could not say that it is due to fate that children happen not to receive baptism. And when they ventured to assert that infants are free from sin, they were rightly condemned.[274] But when the question is raised about the discrimination of all mankind, one cannot very well exclude infants from all mankind. And since, too, He who is Truth, said of all men of all ages indiscriminately, *The Son of man is come to seek and to save that which was lost,*[275] they try in vain to sound the depth of grace which is unsearchable, with their "free will," and to find in human merits the reason for the election of all those who happen to be chosen. Though they did advance many silly and false statements about the will and judgment of adults,[276] they fail to account for the discrimination among infants; and they cannot boast of having given a satisfactory answer to a question that concerns all men,[277] but which they fail to solve for all.


CHAPTER 23

*All human merit from the beginning of faith to final*
*perseverance is a divine gift. This is shown*
*first regarding faith.*

The rich variety and the greatness of divine grace [278] show that the theories of those men are false even when they speak of the wills of adults.[279] The evidence of the inspired writings refutes their opinion. If we wanted to quote all these texts, our dissertation would never end. We shall, however, mention some that come to our mind. Our purpose is to show as far as is necessary that a man's merit from the beginning of faith to final perseverance [280] is a gift and a work of God.

To begin with faith, which is the source of good will and of righteous actions—the Apostle Paul explains whence it springs when he gives thanks to God for the faith of the

Romans in these words: *First, I give thanks to my God, through Jesus Christ, for you all, because your faith is spoken of in the whole world.*[281] When writing to the Ephesians, too, he says: *Wherefore I also, hearing of your faith that is in the Lord Jesus and of your love towards all the saints, cease not to give thanks for you, making commemoration of you in my prayers, that the God of our Lord Jesus Christ, the Father of glory, may give unto you the spirit of wisdom and of revelation, in view of the knowledge of Him: the eyes of your heart enlightened, that you may know what the hope is of His calling, what are the riches of the glory of His inheritance in the saints.*[282] Likewise, thanking God for the faith of the Colossians, he says: *We give thanks to God and the Father of our Lord Jesus Christ, praying always for you, hearing your faith in Christ Jesus and the love which you have towards all saints, for the hope that is laid up for you in heaven. . . .*[283] And he explains what other good things he is asking for them in his prayers to the same Author of all good things, saying: *Therefore we also, from the day that we heard it, cease not to pray for you and to beg that you may be filled with the knowledge of His will, in all wisdom and spiritual understanding: that you may walk worthy of God, pleasing Him; being fruitful in every good work and increasing in the knowledge of God; strengthened with all might, according to the power of His glory, in all patience and long-suffering with joy.*[284] In the same sense, to the Thessalonians with their ardent spirit of faith and love, he says: *We give thanks to God always for you all: making a remembrance of you in our prayers without ceasing, being mindful of the work of your faith and labour and charity and of the enduring of the hope of our Lord Jesus Christ before God and our Father.*[285] And further: *Therefore, we also give thanks to God without ceasing: because, that when you had received of us the word of the hearing of God, you received it, not as the word of men, but (as it is indeed) the word of God, who worketh in you that have believed.*[286]

Could there be a fuller or more evident proof that the faith of the believers is a gift of God, than these thanks given to God precisely because they who heard the word of God in man's preaching did not disbelieve in it as coming from a man's mouth, but believed in God speaking through men and producing in their hearts this very faith? In his Second Epistle to the same Thessalonians the Apostle speaks about the faith of those who are advancing in Christ, in these words: *We are bound to give thanks always to God for you, brethren, as it is fitting, because your faith groweth exceedingly and the charity of every one of you towards each other aboundeth. So that we ourselves also glory in you in the churches of God, for your patience and faith in all your persecutions and tribulations which you endure for an example of the just judgment of God, that you may be counted worthy of the kingdom of God, for which you also suffer.*[287]

The Apostle Peter also preaches that faith comes from God, and writes: *Knowing that you were not redeemed with corruptible things, as gold and silver, from your vain conversation of the tradition of your fathers, but with the precious blood of Christ Jesus, as of a lamb unspotted and undefiled, foreknown indeed before the foundation of the world, but manifested in the last times for you; who through Him are faithful to God who raised Him up from the dead and hath given Him glory, that your faith and*

6 14

*hope might be in the Lord.*[288] The same again in his Second Epistle speaks of receiving the faith in these words: *Simon Peter, servant and apostle of Jesus Christ, to them that have obtained equal faith with us through the justice of our Lord and Saviour Jesus Christ.*[289]

The Apostle John indicates very clearly the source of the spirit of faith, when he says: *Every spirit which confesseth that Jesus is come in the flesh, is of God; and every spirit that dissolveth Jesus is not of God. And this is Antichrist.*[290] He also says that only a man who has the spirit of truth accepts the Gospel. *We*, says he, *are of God. He that knoweth God heareth us. He that is not of God, heareth us not. By this we know the spirit of truth and the spirit of error.*[291]

Again, in the Acts of the Apostles we hear Peter the Apostle proclaiming that faith comes from the Lord Jesus Christ. He says: *This man, whom you see and know, hath His name strengthened. And the faith which is by Him hath given this perfect soundness in the sight of you all.*[292] In the same narrative we read of the faith of Lydia whom the Lord singled out among the women that heard the Gospel to open her heart: *And upon the Sabbath day we went forth without the gate by a river side, where it seemed that there was prayer; and sitting down, we spoke to the women that were assembled. And a certain woman named Lydia, a seller of purple, of the city of Thyatira, one that worshipped God, did hear: whose heart the Lord opened to attend to those things which were said by Paul.*[293]

The word of the Truth itself confirms that faith does not originate in human wisdom but in a divine inspiration; for the Lord said to His disciples: *But whom do you say that I am? Simon Peter answered and said: Thou art Christ, the Son of the Living God. And Jesus answering said to him: Blessed art thou, Simon, Bar-Jona, because flesh and blood hath not revealed it to thee, but my Father who is in heaven.*[294]

The Apostle Paul preaches that this same faith is given in a measure determined by the will of the Giver: *For I say by the grace that is given me, to all that are among you not to be more wise than it behoveth to be wise, but to be wise unto sobriety, according as God hath divided to every one the measure of faith.*[295] He also writes that it is God who gives unity in the true faith and concord in praising God. *Now,* he says, *the God of patience and comfort grant you to be of one mind, one towards another, according to Jesus Christ, that with one mind and with one mouth you may glorify God and the Father of our Lord Jesus Christ.*[296] And further: *Now the God of hope fill you with all joy and peace in believing, that you may abound in hope and in the power of the Holy Spirit.*[297] This text teaches that not only faith, but also joy and peace and abundance of hope cannot be had except through the power of the Holy Spirit.

Again, when writing to the Ephesians the Apostle mentions the riches of grace which returns good for evil; and, speaking of faith which is not our conquest but God's gift, he says: *But God, who is rich in mercy, for His exceeding charity wherewith He loved us even when we were dead in sins, hath quickened us up together in Christ, by whose grace we are saved, and hath raised us up together and hath made us sit together in the heavenly places, through Christ Jesus. . . . For by grace you are saved through faith, and that not of yourselves, for it is the gift of God; not of works, that no man may glory. For we are His handiwork, created in Christ Jesus in good works which God hath prepared that we should walk in them.*[298] The new creation, then, that rises from grace causes them who are God's handiwork and who through a heavenly birth are established in Christ, not to indulge in an idle life nor to yield to slothfulness, but rather to advance from virtue to virtue along the path of good works. That is the meaning of being "His handiwork," of being changed from the old creation to the new, of being reformed from the likeness of the earthly man into the likeness of the heavenly one. This may be done visibly through such as cooperate with grace, or in a hidden manner through the ministry of the Spirit. In either case beginning, increase, and completion are the work of Him whose husbandry, whose building,[298a] whose handiwork we are.

CHAPTER 24

*Grace is the source of all good in man. Faith is given unasked and enables us to obtain in prayer all other blessings.*

This evidence from Scripture—and we could gather many other texts—demonstrates abundantly, I think, that faith which justifies a sinner cannot be had except for God's gift, and that it is not a reward for previous merits.[299] Rather is it given that it may be a source of merit, and while it is itself given unprayed for, the prayers it inspires obtain [300] all other favours. To prove this some texts out of

many must be cited which will show the bounty of grace
in the variety of its gifts. To begin with, it is God who
causes a man to choose God's way or to rise from a fall,
as we read in the Psalm in which David sings: *By the
Lord shall the steps of a man be directed, and he shall like
well His way. When he shall fall, he shall not be bruised,
for the Lord putteth His hand under him.*[301] He also says
that God guides men to come to God: *Send forth Thy
light and Thy truth: they have conducted me and brought
me into Thy holy hill and into Thy tabernacles.*[302] He
says likewise that a man's strength rests in the Lord, and
that God's will takes the initiative in a man's liberation:
*I will keep my strength to Thee, for Thou, God, art my
protector. My God, His will shall prevent me.*[303]

In the Proverbs we also read about wisdom and understanding: *Because the Lord giveth wisdom, and out of
His face cometh knowledge and understanding.*[304] In the
same book again it is stated regarding the dispensations of
God's wisdom without which no actions are righteous:
*Counsel and protection is mine; I am prudence, strength
is mine. By me the kings reign and tyrants by me occupy
the earth.*[305] Again, elsewhere it is said that no one can
walk along the right path except through the Lord's guidance: *The steps of man are guided by the Lord. But who
is the mortal that can understand his own ways?* [306] Elsewhere, again, *Every man seemeth right to himself; but the
Lord guideth the hearts.*[307] And further, *The will is
prepared by the Lord.*[308] Likewise in the same book we
read about human thought and counsel, *There are many
thoughts in the heart of man; but the counsel of the Lord
prevaileth.*[309]

In the Book of Ecclesiastes we find it written that both

to have what we need and to make good use of it is given us by God: *This only is good for man, that he ate and drank, and he showeth the good of his soul in his labour. And of all this I have seen that it comes from God's hand. For who shall eat and be nourished without Him?* [310] Again in the same book we read that the hearts and the works of the just are in God's hand and that they succeed in their pursuits in the measure He grants success: *However much a man shall labour to seek, he shall not find; and whatsoever the wise man shall say that he knoweth, he shall not be able to find. . . . Because all this he has put in my heart and my heart hath seen all this, because just men and wise men and their works are in the hand of God.* [311]

In the Book of Wisdom it is said about the same work of grace: *Because He is also the guide of wisdom and the director of the wise. For in His hands are both we, and our words, and all wisdom, and the knowledge and skill of works.* [312] The same book speaks of continence as being a favour which God bestows on man: *As I knew that I could not otherwise be continent, except God gave it, and this also was a point of wisdom, to know whose gift it was.* [313] The teaching of the Apostle Paul is in agreement with this opinion when he writes, in the First Epistle to the Corinthians: *For I would that all men were even as myself. But every one hath his proper gift from God: one after this manner, another after that.* [314] Our Lord also insinuates the same about the gift of continence as related in the Gospel according to Matthew. When His disciples said, *If the case of a man with his wife be so, it is not expedient to marry,* Jesus answered, *Not all men take this word, but they to whom it is given.* [315] Of the fear of God and of wisdom we read in Ecclesiasticus: *The fear of the Lord is a crown of wisdom, . . . but both are gifts of God.*[316] Also in the same book: *The fear of the Lord hath set itself above all things. Blessed is he to whom it is given to have the fear of God.*[317] Isaias, too, speaks of the spiritual riches of which the Lord is the Author, in these words: *Our salvation cometh with treasures—wisdom, piety, and instruction from the Lord: these are the treasures of justice.*[318] Likewise about the depth of the riches of the wisdom and knowledge of God whose goodness no man's merit can outstrip, he says: *Who hath measured the waters in His hand and weighed the heavens with His palm and the whole earth with the hollow of His hand? Who hath placed the mountains in scales and the hills in a balance? Who hath known the sense of the Lord, or who hath been His counsellor who advised Him? Or with whom hath He consulted, and who hath instructed Him? Or who hath shown Him judgment, or shown Him the way of understanding? Or who hath given Him first, that he would be given in return?* [319] Further, in the Book of Job we read in the same sense the words of the Lord: *Who hath given me before that I should repay him? All things that are under heaven are mine.*[320]

Jeremias, explaining that man receives wisdom from God, states as follows: *I know, O Lord, that the way of a man is not his; neither is it of a man . . . to direct his way.*[321] Again the Lord proclaims through the same Prophet that God operates the conversion of a heart to God, and says: *I will bring them again into this land. And I will build them up again and not pull them down; and I will plant them and not pluck them up. And I will give them a heart to know me, that I am the Lord; and they shall be my people and I will be their God; because they shall return to me with their whole heart.*[322] Baruch also proclaims that knowledge of God comes from God. *And they shall know,* he says, *that I am the Lord their God; and I will give them a heart to understand, and ears to hear.*[323]

In the First Epistle to the Corinthians the Apostle Paul teaches that every good word and every holy action is inspired by the Holy Spirit, without whom we can do nothing that is right. He says: *Wherefore, I give you to understand that no man, speaking by the Spirit of God, saith Anathema to Jesus. And no man can say The Lord Jesus, but by the Holy Spirit. Now there are diversities of graces, but the same Spirit. And there are diversities of ministries, but the same Lord. And there are diversities of operations, but the same God who worketh all in all. And the manifestation of the Spirit is given to every man unto profit. To one indeed, by the Spirit is given the word of wisdom; and to another, the word of knowledge according to the same Spirit; to another, faith in the same Spirit; to another, the grace of healing in the same Spirit; . . . to another, prophecy; to another, the discerning of spirits; to another, diverse kinds of tongues; to another, interpretation of speeches. But all these things one and the same Spirit worketh, dividing to every one according as He will.*[324]

The same Apostle, writing to the Ephesians, states that each one possesses that much of grace as the Lord gives him: *One body and one Spirit: as you are called in one hope of your calling. One Lord, one faith, one baptism. One God and Father of all, who is above all men, and above all things, and in us all. But to every one of us is given grace according to the measure of the giving of Christ. Wherefore He saith: "Ascending on high, He led captivity captive; He gave gifts to men."* [325] The same again in his Second Epistle to the Corinthians says that we are not able even to conceive a spiritual thought except with God's grace: *And such confidence we have, through Christ, towards God. Not that we are sufficient to think anything of ourselves, as of ourselves; but our sufficiency is from God. Who also hath made us fit ministers of the new testament, not in the letter, but in the spirit: for the letter killeth, but the spirit quickeneth.*[326] And again in the same epistle he teaches that God's grace gives efficacy and sufficiency to good works. He states: *And God is able to make all grace abound in you, that ye through all having sufficiently in all things, may abound to every good work, as it is written: "He hath dispersed abroad, He hath given to the poor; His justice remaineth for ever." And He that ministereth seed to the sower, will both give you bread to eat . . . and increase the growth of the fruits of your justice, that being enriched in all things, you may abound unto all simplicity.*[327]

When writing to the Ephesians, the Apostle teaches them that all good things by which man pleases God are His gifts, and that they have to beg Him to bestow them on all who have not received them yet. He says: *For this cause I bow my knees to the Father of our Lord Jesus Christ, of whom all paternity in heaven and earth is named, that He would grant you might according to the riches of His glory, that you might be strengthened by His Spirit in the inward man; that Christ may dwell by faith in your hearts; that, being rooted and confirmed in charity, you may be able to comprehend with all the saints, what is the breadth and length, height and depth; to know also the charity of Christ, which surpasseth all knowledge; that you may be filled unto all the fulness of God. Now to Him who is able to do all things more abundantly than we desire or understand, according to the power that worketh in us: to Him be glory in the Church and in Christ Jesus, world without end. Amen.*[328]

That the author of all good is God whose gifts, neither uncertain nor changeable, flow from His eternal will, the Apostle James states as follows: *Do not err, my dear brethren. Every best gift and every perfect gift is from above, coming down from the Father of lights, with whom there is no change nor shadow of alteration. For of His own will hath He begotten us by the word of truth, that we might be some beginning of His creature.*[329] And the prophet Zacharias agrees with him when he says: *And the Lord will save His people in that day as sheep; for holy stones shall be rolled over His land. For whatever is good is His, and whatever is best, comes from Him.*[330]

In the Gospel according to Matthew it is said that knowledge and understanding are gifts of God which He grants to whomsoever He pleases: *Then His disciples came and said to Him: Why speakest Thou to them in parables? But He answered and said to them: Because to you it is given to know the mysteries of the kingdom of heaven; but to them it is not given.*[331] John the Evangelist also proclaims that no man possesses any good which he has not received from on high. *A man,* he says, *cannot receive anything unless it be given him from heaven.*[332] In the same Gospel the Truth itself teaches that no one comes to the Son except drawn to Him by the Father, for it is God who bestows on any man that is to come to Him, both understanding and willingness. He says: *No man can come to me, except the Father, who hath sent me, draw him; and I will raise him up in the last day. For it is written in the Prophets: "And they shall all be taught of God." Every one that hath heard of the Father and hath learned, cometh to me;* [333] and further, *Therefore did I say to you that no man can come to me, unless it be given him by my Father.* [334]

The authority of Sacred Scripture confirms that a divine gift and a divine help is necessary for man to make progress in faith and good works and to persevere in them till the end. Thus the Apostle Paul, writing to the Philippians, says: *Being confident of this very thing: that He who hath begun a good work in you, will perfect it unto the day of Christ Jesus.* [335] Some one wanted to explain this text so as to prove from it his own perverse teaching; he wanted the text which reads, *who hath begun in you,* to be understood as though it read, *who hath begun "from" you.* [336] Thus he attributed both the beginning and the completion of a work not to God but to man, whose will would be responsible for such a beginning and completion. [337] But in the same epistle the great preacher of grace shatters this most insane pride, saying: *In nothing be ye terrified by the adversaries: which to them is a cause of perdition, but to you of salvation, and this from God. For unto you it is given for Christ, not only to believe in Him, but also to suffer for Him.* [338] And again he says: *With fear and trembling work out your salvation. For it is God who worketh in you, both to will and to work, according to His good will.* [339] Likewise in his First Epistle to the Thessalonians he teaches that the beginning, progress, and perfection of every virtue come from

God, saying: *Now God himself and our Father and the Lord Jesus direct our way unto you. And may the Lord multiply you and make you abound in charity towards one another and towards all men, as we do also towards you. To confirm your hearts without blame, in holiness, before God and our Father, at the coming of our Lord Jesus Christ, with all His saints.*[340] When writing to the Corinthians, too, and declaring that progress and perseverance in every virtue is a gift of God, he says: *I give thanks to my God always for you, for the grace of God that is given you in Christ Jesus: that in all things you are made rich in Him, in all utterance and wisdom; as the testimony of Christ was confirmed in you, so that nothing is wanting to you in any grace, waiting for the manifestation of our Lord Jesus Christ. Who also will confirm you unto the end without crime for the day of the coming of the Lord Jesus Christ.*[341]

Again, writing to the Romans, he speaks about the charity of Christ by which He makes unconquerable those whom He loves, that is—makes them persevere till the end (for, what else is it to persevere but not to be overcome by temptation?): *Who shall separate us from the love of Christ? Shall tribulation, or distress, or persecution, or famine, or nakedness, or danger, or the sword? (As it is written: "For Thy sake, we are put to death all the day long. We are accounted as sheep for the slaughter.") But in all these things we overcome through Him that hath loved us.*[342] Likewise to the Corinthians he speaks about the victory won by Christ: *The sting of death is sin, and the power of sin is the law. But thanks be to God, who hath given us the victory through Jesus Christ our Lord.*[343] To the Thessalonians, too, he states about perseverance as a gift of God: *And may the God of peace Himself sanctify you in all things: that your whole spirit and soul and body may be preserved blameless for the coming of our Lord Jesus Christ. He is faithful who hath called you, who will also do it.*[344] To the Thessalonians again, to explain that all good either in deeds or in words, and perseverance in it, is a gift of God, he says: *Now our Lord Jesus Christ Himself and God our Father, who hath loved us and hath given us everlasting consolation and good hope in grace, exhort your hearts and confirm you in every good work and word. For the rest, brethren, pray for us, that the word of the Lord may run and may be glorified, even as among you; and that we may be delivered from importunate and evil men, for not all men have faith. But God is faithful, who will strengthen and keep you from evil.*[345]

Let us also listen to what the Apostle Peter teaches about the source of our strength for perseverance; he says: *But the God of all grace, who hath called us unto His eternal glory in Christ Jesus, after you have suffered a little, will Himself perfect you and confirm you and establish you; to whom belongs strength and power, for ever and ever. Amen.*[346] And the Apostle John, explaining that the victory of the saints is the work of God living in the saints, says: *You are of God, little children, and have overcome the world; because greater is He that is in you, than he that is in the world.*[347] And the same again: *Whatsoever is born of God, overcometh the world. And this is the victory which overcometh the world: our faith.*[348] In the Gospel according to Luke it is brought out that it is God who gives perseverance in faith, in these words: *And Jesus said to Peter: Simon, Simon, behold*

*Satan hath desired to have you, that he might sift you as
wheat. But I have prayed for thee, that thy faith fail not:
and thou, being converted, confirm thy brethren, and pray
lest you enter into temptation.*[349]

Also in the Gospel of John we read the Truth saying of
Christ's sheep whom no one can snatch from His hand:
*But you do not believe, because you are not of my sheep.
My sheep hear my voice, and I know them; and they follow me. And I give them life everlasting; and they shall
not perish for ever, and no man shall pluck them out of
my hand.*[350] Likewise in the same Gospel we hear from
the mouth of the Lord Himself, when He speaks of those
whom the Father gives to the Son and who all come to the
Son and of whom no one is lost: *All that the Father
giveth to me, cometh to me; and him that cometh to me,
I will not cast him out. Because I am come down from
heaven, not to do my will, but the will of Him that sent
me, the Father, . . . that of all that He hath given me, I
should lose nothing, but raise it up again in the last
day.*[351]

CHAPTER 25

*The problem why one man receives grace rather
than another we cannot solve; the answer
does not lie with their free will.*

There are[352] many other passages in the canonical
Scriptures which we have omitted intentionally for brevity's sake. The texts we have cited are not few, neither

are they equivocal or unimportant. They state quite plainly that whatever has to do with merit unto eternal life, can neither be begun nor increased nor be completed without God's grace. On the contrary, all pride that boasts of free will, bows down before the famous and unanswerable question of the Apostle: *For who distinguishes thee? Or what hast thou that thou hast not received? And if thou hast received, why dost thou glory, as if thou hadst not received it?* [353] Accordingly, this profound problem of which we confess with the awe-struck Apostle [354] that it cannot be fathomed, is not solved by appealing to the acts of the free will.[355] For, although it lies in a man's power to reject what is good, yet, unless it is given him, he is unable by himself to choose this good.[356] The power to do the former was contracted by our nature with original sin; but nature has to receive the ability to do the latter from grace.

Nature is the same in all men, guilty and wretched in all before its reconciliation. Not all men are justified and only a certain part of them are set apart from the reprobate by Him who *is come to seek and save that which was lost.*[357] But why this is so, our human intellect can in no way find out. You may point ever so much to the wickedness of the unbelievers, their resistence to God's grace: will this prove that they to whom grace is given have merited it? Or has this same grace, which subjected to itself whom it pleased, remained powerless to convert also them that have remained unconvertible? Those who were won by grace had the same nature as they who were left in their hardness of heart. To the first, amazing grace granted what it pleased, to the second, just truth rendered their due. Actually, God's judgments are still more inscrutable when His grace chooses the elect than when His justice punishes the reprobate.

But we may not leave the impression that the doctrine of our faith [358] according to which we devoutly believe that God wills all men to be saved through the recognition of the truth, is weakened by what we have explained and proved about the effects of grace. [359] For that reason we must try to show, with the help of Christ, that this doctrine stands unassailable. But because an amount of research is necessary for what is a formidable task, let us undertake the discussion that is still to follow with the beginning of our Second Book.

# BOOK TWO

## CHAPTER 1

*Three points are certain in this matter: God wills
all men to be saved, the knowledge of truth
and salvation is due to grace, and
God's judgments are inscrutable.*

If we give up completely all wrangling that springs up
in the heat of immoderate disputes, it will be clear that
we must hold for certain three points concerning the
problem on which we begin our Second Book.[1] First, we
must confess that God wills all men to be saved and to
come to the knowledge of truth.[2] Secondly, there can be
no doubt that all who actually come to the knowledge[3]
of the truth and to salvation, do so not in virtue of their
own merits but of the efficacious help of divine grace.[4]
Thirdly, we must admit that human understanding is
unable to fathom the depths of God's judgments, and we
ought not to inquire why He who wishes all men to be
saved does not in fact save all.[5] For if we do not search
into what we cannot know,[6] then we shall have no difficulty in reconciling the first point with the second, but
we shall be able to preach and to believe them both with
the security of an undisturbed faith. God indeed in whom
there is no injustice[7] and *all of whose ways are mercy and
truth*,[8] is the beneficent Creator of all men and their just
Ruler. He condemns no one without guilt and saves no
one for his merits. When He chastises the guilty, He
punishes our demerits, and when He makes us just, He

bestows of His own gifts.[9] Thus *the mouth is stopped of them that speak wicked things* [10] and *God is justified in His words and overcomes when He is judged.*[11] The condemned cannot complain in justice that they did not deserve punishment, nor can the justified truthfully claim that they have merited grace.

## CHAPTER 2

*Scripture teaches that God wills all men to be saved.*

We must not profane with our human dialectics the texts quoted from the divine Scriptures [12] to explain what grace is; that would be to drag so many clear and concordant statements into the uncertainty of a misleading interpretation. In the same way, no argumentation to the contrary must defile what we find in the same body of Scripture about the salvation of all men. Rather, the more difficult is its understanding the more praiseworthy will the faith be that believes.[13] That assent is indeed very strong whose motive is derived from authority as a sufficient proof of truth, even though the *why* of things remain hidden.

Let us, then, carefully examine the behest which our Lord makes to the preachers of the gospel. According to Matthew, He says: *All power is given to me in heaven and in earth. Going, therefore, teach ye all nations, baptizing them in the name of the Father and of the Son and of the Holy Spirit, teaching them to observe all things whatso-*

*ever I have commanded you. And behold I am wtih you all days, even to the consummation of the world.*[14] According to Mark, He speaks thus to the same Apostles: *Go ye into the world and preach the gospel to every creature, and he that believeth and is baptized shall be saved; but he that believeth not shall be condemned.*[15]

Does this command make a difference between any peoples or any individuals? No, He welcomed no one for his merits, singled out no one for his birth, made no distinction with anyone because of his social state. The gospel of the Cross of Christ was extended to all men without exception. And that no one should consider the ministry of the preachers as but a merely human enterprise, He said, *Behold I am with you all days, even to the consummation of the world.*[16] That is, when you will go like sheep in the midst of wolves,[17] do not be afraid on account of your weakness; have confidence in my power, for I shall not forsake you in this great mission till the end of the world. Not that you will have nothing to suffer; but what is much greater, I shall give you strength that you may not be overcome by any cruelty of savage tyrants. For you will preach with my power; and through me it will come about that from among your opponents and persecutors sons of Abraham will be raised up from the very stones.[18] I shall instil my doctrine, I shall accomplish my promise. *For they will deliver you up in councils and they will scourge you in their synagogues. And you shall stand before kings and governors for my sake, for a testimony to them and to the Gentiles. But when they shall deliver you up, take no thought how or what to speak. . . . For it is not you that speak, but the Spirit of your Father that speaketh in you. The brother also shall deliver up the brother to death, and the father the son; and "the children shall raise up against their parents" and shall put them to death. And you shall be hated by all men, for my name's sake. But he that shall persevere unto the end, he shall be saved.*[19]

*Therefore,* as the Apostle says, *the grace of God our Saviour hath appeared to all men;*[20] and yet the ministers of His grace were hated by all. There were those who hated on the one hand, and on the other, those who were oppressed by the hatred of their persecutors; but neither group was excluded in the term *"all* men," even though the class of the rebels suffered the loss of their salvation, while the faithful in their privileged condition were accounted a totality.[21] For the Apostle John says: *But if any man sin, we have an advocate with the Father, Jesus Christ the Just. And He is the propitiation for our sins; and not for our sins only, but also for those of the whole world.*[22]

CHAPTER 3

*We cannot know why God decreed to delay the call of some nations.*

We find the sign of a great and ineffable mystery[23] in the fact that the same preachers to whom our Lord said, *Go ye into the whole world and preach the Gospel to every creature,*[24] had first been commanded: *Go ye not into the way of the Gentiles, and into the city of the Samaritans enter ye not. But go ye rather to the lost sheep of the house of Israel.*[25] For though the call of the Gospel was addressed to all men, and the Lord willed *all men to be saved and to come to the knowledge of truth,*[26] yet He had not taken from Himself the power over His own rulings so that His decree would come into effect otherwise than He had decided in His hidden and just judgment.[27] We can, therefore, have no just reason for murmuring or for insolent complaints, since it is evident that what God has decreed had not to happen in any other manner than He decided. At a later time when the Lord Jesus was already sitting in the glory of God the Father and when the preachers of God's word were discharging their mission, the Apostles intended to preach the Gospel in Asia, but *they were forbidden by the Holy Spirit.*[28] And when they attempted to go into Bithynia, the Spirit of Jesus suffered them not; [29] not because grace was refused to those peoples, but, as far as we can see, it was only delayed. In fact, later the Christian faith grew from strength to strength among them as well.

We do not see the reason why God delayed their call. Even so, this historical fact is an object lesson. We learn that among the things which God ordinarily promises, designs, or orders, He makes some exceptions to the common laws, and in His wisdom ordains them in a more mysterious manner. I think it is His purpose to bring out more strikingly the mysterious clarity of His design by contrast with some things veiled in obscurity.[30] He does not want our investigation to become slothful when we find the truth without much effort, as when we are lulled into security by familiar objects unless something unusual crops up to awaken us. At any rate, we know that these incomprehensible delays of enlightenment take place, and that meanwhile many actually die in unbelief, not only among the distant nations of infidels, but even in the cities of the faithful in numerous houses and families as long as they who will eventually be Christians are adverse to the Christian faith. For many will love what they now hate, and will preach what they now refuse to accept.

Faced with these facts, who will tell the querulous and the curious why the Sun of Justice [31] still does not rise for some peoples; why the Truth that will shine on them one day, still keeps back its rays from their hearts shrouded in darkness? [32] Why are future converts allowed to continue in their errors for so long? Why are aged men refused during a long lifetime the light which they see in the end? Why do parents not yet have the faith when their children already believe in Christ? Again, why the disparity of devout parents having a wicked offspring? But it is at God's own behest that prayers are offered for all men every day [33] to Him who gives to all the beginning of faith and progress in it: therefore, we must know and understand that when He hears these prayers, His mercy grants a gratuitous gift; and when He does not, then His judgment remains truthful.

## CHAPTER 4

*In past ages God's goodness drew all men to His worship
through things created, but Israel in a special
way through the Law and the Prophets.*

Not even in the past ages [34] was the world without
this same grace, which after the Resurrection of our Lord
Jesus Christ has spread everywhere and of which Scripture says, *Thy lightnings enlightened the world.*[35] It
is true that God's special care and mercy chose the people
of Israel as His own, while all the other nations were
left *to walk in their own ways,*[36] that is, to live according
to their own choosing. Yet the eternal goodness of their
Creator did not turn away from them so as not to ad-
monish them with some tokens of His own, of their duty
to know and fear Him. Indeed, the heavens and the
earth, the sea and every creature that man can see or
know, is for the service of mankind; and chiefly for this
purpose, that the rational beings, when contemplating
so many beautiful things, enjoying so many good gifts,
receiving so many favours, must needs learn to worship
and love the Author of them all. The Spirit of God *in
whom we live and move and are,*[37] fills the whole world.
For although *salvation is far from sinners,*[38] yet nothing
is devoid of His saving presence and power.

Thus, as the Prophet says, *The earth is full of the
Lord's mercy,*[39] which has never forsaken any ages or
any generations. He ever shows His Providence by which
He governs and sustains the whole universe when He

rules and feeds all living creatures. In the eternity of His immutable design He has settled what He would dispense at each particular age and by which gifts and mysteries [40] He would unfold the inscrutable and unsearchable rhythm of His multiform grace. The very wealth of His grace which in these times has flowed over to the Gentiles must not make us forget the grace which under the Law bedewed Israel alone, and the present riches do not dispense us from believing in the past scarcity. Likewise God's particular care by which He guided the sons of the Patriarchs in the right path must not make one fancy that the ruling of the divine mercy was withheld from all other men. Compared with the chosen people, they may look like castaways, but in fact they never were denied God's manifest and hidden mercies. Indeed, we read in the Acts of the Apostles that the Apostles Paul and Barnabas said to the Lycaonians: *Ye men, why do ye these things? We also are mortals, men like unto you, preaching to you to be converted from these vain things to the living God, who made the heaven and the earth and the sea and all things that are in them; who in times past suffered all nations to walk in their own ways. Nevertheless, He left not Himself without testimony, doing them good, from heaven giving rains and fruitful seasons, filling our hearts with food and gladness.* [41]

Now, what else is this testimony, always at the Lord's command and never silent about His goodness and power, [42] except the unspeakable beauty of the whole world and the rich and orderly dispensation of His countless [43] mercies? These offered to the hearts of men tables, as it were, of the Eternal Law where they could read in the pages of the created things and the volumes of the unfolding ages the universal and common doctrine God was teaching them. The heavens and all the things in the heavens, the sea and the earth and all that is in them in the perfect harmony of their beauty and order, proclaim the glory of God and in ceaseless preaching speak of the majesty of their Maker. In spite of all this, the greater number of men who were left to walk in the ways of their own choice, did not understand nor follow this Law. The vivifying fragrance that breathed life became for them *a deadly odour unto death*,[44] so that we learned also of these testimonies of the visible world that *the letter killeth, but the spirit quickeneth*.[45] Thus, what the promulgation of the Law and the preaching of the Prophets did for Israel, that the testimony of the whole creation with all the wonders of God's goodness wrought at all times for all nations.

CHAPTER 5

*The Gentiles who pleased God were singled out by a gratuitous spirit of faith.*

Within the people of Israel which was guided by both these teachings—of things created and of the Law and Prophets—no one could be justified except through grace in a spirit of faith.[46] Who, then, would doubt that all men, at all times, from whatever nation, who were able to please God, had been singled out by the breath of God's grace? [47] That grace, it is true, was more sparingly given [48] and less apparent among the Gentiles; but it was not denied to any nation—always one and the same in its power, though varying in measure; immutable in its design, though multiform in its effects.[49]

## CHAPTER 6

*Even in our times grace is not given to all
men in the same measure.*

Even in our own day when streams of ineffable gifts
flood the whole world, grace is not bestowed on all men
in the same measure and intensity. Though the ministers of the word and of God's grace preach the same truth
to all and address to all the same exhortations, yet this is
*God's husbandry* and *God's building,* and it is He whose
power invisibily acts and gives growth to what they build
or cultivate.[50] The Apostle attests this in these words:
*What, then, is Apollo, and what is Paul? The ministers
of Him whom you have believed; and to every one as the
Lord hath given. I have planted, Apollo watered; but
God hath given the increase. Therefore, neither he that
planteth is anything, nor he that watereth; but God that
giveth the increase. Now, he that planteth and he that
watereth, are one. And every man shall receive his own
reward, according to his own labour. For we are God's
coadjutors; you are God's husbandry, you are God's
building.*[51]

In this husbandry and this building every man is a
helper, a workman and a minister, in the measure of the
Lord's gift. And they who are tended by the toil of the
ministers, progress in the very measure in which the
Author of all growth raises them; for in the Lord's field
the plants are not all uniformly developed nor is there

one kind of plants only. Again, although the structure
of the whole temple makes for all the beauty that it has,
yet the places and functions of the stones that go into
it, are not the same for all; just as in one body all members have not the same function, as the Apostle says—
*But now God hath set the members, and every one of
them as it hath pleased Him.*[52]


## CHAPTER 7

*The inequality of the divine gifts does not come
from the merits of preceding works,
but from God's liberality.*

The same Teacher explains from where all the members of the body derive their fitness, function, and beauty
in these words: *Wherefore, I give you to understand that
no man, speaking by the Spirit of God, saith Anathema
to Jesus. And no man can say The Lord Jesus, but by the
Holy Spirit. Now, there are diversities of graces, but the
same Spirit. And there are diversities of ministers, but the
same Lord. And there are diversities of operations, but
the same God who worketh all in all. And the manifestation of the Spirit is given to every man unto profit. To
one indeed, by the Spirit is given the word of wisdom;
and to another, the word of knowledge according to the
same Spirit; to another, faith in the same Spirit; to another, the grace of healing in the same Spirit; to another,
the working of miracles; to another prophecy; to another,
the discerning of spirits; to another, diverse kinds of*

*tongues; to another, interpretation of speeches. But all
these things one and the same Spirit worketh, dividing to
every one according as He will.*[53] Considering this crystal-
clear preaching of the Teacher of the Gentiles, who could
find a reason or a pretext to doubt that we receive the
seed of all virtues from God? Who but a consummate
fool would complain of the differences in the divine gifts,
or fancy that it is due to unequally distributed merits
when the divine liberality does not give the same graces
to all? For if the distribution of His favours were regulated by the merits of the antecedent works of men, then
the Apostle would not end his list of divine gifts with the
conclusion, *But all these things, one and the same Spirit
worketh, dividing to every one according as He will.*[54] If
in this passage he had wanted to say that merit is the
determining factor, he would have said, "dividing to each
according as they deserve"; just as He promised those who
plant and water, the reward of their toil by saying, *And
every man shall receive his own reward, according to his
own labour.*[55]

CHAPTER 8

*Every one receives with no merit on his part the means
of gaining merit. Having received grace, he is
expected to increase this gift through
Him who gives the increase.*

Every one receives with no merit on his part the means
of gaining merit, and before he has done any work whatever, he is given the dignity [56] thanks to which his work

will deserve a reward. This fact may also be gathered from the teaching of the Gospel truth, where it is said in the parable: *A man going into a far country called his servants and delivered to them his substance; and to one he gave five talents, and to another two, and to another one, to each one according to his proper ability* [57]—that is, according to his own innate ability and not according to his own deserts. For it is one thing to be able to work and another to work, one thing to be able to have charity and another to have it, one thing to be capable of continence, justice, wisdom and another to be continent, just, and wise. And so not every man that can be remade is actually remade, and not every man who can be healed is actually restored to health; for only the possibility of restoration or healing is given with nature, but it is grace that actually remakes or heals.[58] Finally, when the distributor of his goods entrusted an unequal number of talents to his servants according to their abilities which he foresaw,[59] he was not giving them a reward for merit but material to work with. On the two alert and enterprising servants he not only bestowed high praise but he also ordered them to enter into the eternal joy of their Lord.[60] But he punished the lazy life and listless negligence of the third servant so as not only to disgrace him with reproach and censure, but to deprive him of the share he had received.[61] For, as he had not practised charity, he deserved to lose a faith that bore no fruit in him.

In the discourse that follows and which exposes very clearly the procedure of the future judgment, we read that when the Son of man shall sit upon the seat of His majesty and all the nations shall be gathered before it,[62]

He will place some on His right hand and others on His left. Those at His right He will praise for their works of charity, while to those on His left He will make no other reproach than their neglect of mercy and kindness.[63] They also had received the faith but they did not practise charity; they will be condemned not for not having preserved, but for not having increased the gift they had received.[64] For, though all good things are gifts of God, yet some are granted unasked in order [65] that with these, men may pursue what they have not yet been given. The seed that is cast into the earth is not sown in order that it should remain there alone, but that it may bear fruit and multiply.[66] Its growth, however, comes from Him *who giveth the increase.*[67] And when the living earth of the rational soul has been fertilised by the rain of grace, it is able to increase, as it is expected to do, the gifts it has received.[68]

CHAPTER 9

*We must not seek the reason why God dispenses His grace differently in different ages.*

We have, I believe—with the Lord's help—treated this whole question satisfactorily. Let us, then, after this digression return to our subject, namely, to the consideration of the differences we find in the effects and gifts of divine grace.[69] *The depth of the riches of the wisdom and of the knowledge of God,* whose *judgments are inscrutable and whose ways unsearchable,*[70] has always so tempered His mercy and His justice that according to the most hidden decree of His eternal design He did not wish to give equal measures of grace at all times to all generations or to all individual men. In fact, He chose to help in one way those men whom He invited to His knowledge through the testimony of the heavens and the earth. In another way He chose to help those of whom He took care not only with the service of created things, but also with the doctrine of the Law, the oracles of the Prophets, the language of miracles, and the help of the angels.

But He has shown His mercy for all men in a far more extraordinary manner when the Son of God became the Son of man, so that He could be found by those who did not seek Him and be seen by those who did not call upon Him.[71] Since then the glory of the race of Israel shines not in one people only. To Abraham a numerous posterity is born among all nations under the heavens. The promised heritage falls no longer to the sons of the flesh, but to the sons of the promise.[72] The great parsimony in bestowing grace which in the past ages befell all other nations, is now the lot of the Jewish people. Yet, when the fulness of the Gentiles will have come in, then a flood of the same waters of grace is promised for their dry hearts.[73] Who will tell the reasons and motives of these differences within one and the same grace when Sacred Scripture is silent about them? When the Apostle Paul stopped in his knowledge and discussion of this problem and gave way to utter astonishment,[74] who would be so presumptuous as to believe that he could try and explain it rather than admire it in silence? [75]

CHAPTER 10

*Throughout the centuries God's mercy provided food for the bodies of men and help for their souls.*

Let us, then, with patience and in peace of soul remain ignorant of a secret that is withheld from our human knowledge.[76] We must not, however, because we cannot penetrate into what is closed to us, fail to enter into that which lies open to us. For many evidences from the divine Scriptures and the uninterrupted experience of all ages have made it clear that God's just mercy and merciful justice never ceased to provide food for the bodies of men and direction and help for their minds. At all times *He has rained upon the good and the bad and made His sun rise upon the just and the unjust.*[77] At all times He has given the life-giving air, regulated the alternations of day and night, granted fertility to the fields, growth to the seeds, and fecundity for the propagation of mankind. If at times He withdrew any of these things, then He meant to chastise with fatherly correction the unwillingness and sloth of men who misused them, intending that in adversity they should seek His mercy when in prosperity they forgot the fear of His justice.

Finally, if we go back to the very beginning of the world, we shall find that the Spirit of God was the guide of all the saints who lived before the deluge and who were on account of His guidance called sons of God; because, as the Apostle says, *Whosoever are led by the Spirit of God, they are the sons of God.*[78] When these men paid no attention to the religion of their fathers and contracted forbidden marriages with the reprobate,[79] and when they were judged worthy of extermination because of their wicked alliances, then the Lord said, *My Spirit shall not remain with these men because they are flesh.*[80] Hence it is clear that this people whose history we find narrated there in chronological order, was spiritual at first when their wills were guided by the Holy Spirit,[81] who ruled them in such a manner as not to take away from them the possibility of falling into sin. As long as this people left this power unused, they did not abandon God nor were they forsaken by Him. They were then like the man of whom it is said, *Happy he that could have transgressed, and hath not transgressed.*[82] As long, then, as the people remained united with God, they did so with a will that God inspired and guided, as we read, *For the will is prepared by the Lord.*[83]

CHAPTER 11

*Men acquire slowly and little by little what God's liberality has decreed to give them.*

But this preparation does not always follow the same process or keep the same rhythm. Because the effects and the gifts of grace appear in many ways and in countless variations, within the several kinds of gifts there are still different degrees and unequal measures. The offshoots of herbs and trees that spring from the earth are not all of one species or of one kind, but one and all they are shaped according to the pattern of their kind and the properties of their species; and they do not have their full shapeliness as soon as they appear, but develop gradually and orderly till they reach their own individual size through successive stages of growth. In the same way the seeds of divine graces and the plants of the virtues do not spring forth in the field of all human hearts in that perfection which they will acquire later; and you do not easily find maturity from the beginning or perfection from the start.[84]

It is true, the action of the God of power and mercy frequently produces marvellous effects, and, without awaiting the time required for a gradual progress, at once plants in some minds all that He wishes to confer upon them. In the loins of Abraham Levi was sanctified [85] and with him the whole house of Aaron and the priestly class was blessed.[86] In Isaac who was conceived according to promise and born against the hope of his aged and sterile parents,[87] the call of all the Gentiles and the fulness of Christ is prefigured. Jacob without any merits to speak for him was beloved and chosen before he was born.[88] To Jeremias was said: *Before I formed thee in the bowels of thy mother, I knew thee; and before thou camest forth out of the womb I sanctified thee.*[89] John, still in the womb of his mother Elizabeth, was filled with the Holy Spirit and leaped up,[90] and that there might be no one greater than him among the sons of women,[91] he awoke to the life of grace before that of nature.

Though other texts of like applicability are not lacking, we pass them over for brevity's sake. But we meet with many more frequent and more numerous cases of men to whom the heavenly bounty grows as its gifts are granted piecemeal: the reasons for granting further gifts

are to arise from those already given. Some men receive
the faith, but are still not without distrust, as, for example, he was aware who said, *I do believe, Lord. Help
my unbelief.*[92] The men also who said, *Lord, increase our
faith,*[93] felt that diffidence was not fully absent from
their hearts. Some do not grasp what they believe, and
many of these remain for a long time confined within
their simplicity. But many soon receive light to understand, yet of these not all have an equally firm and
equally facile power of understanding. And many others
who apparently have both faith and understanding, yet
badly lack charity, and they are unable to cling to what
an enlightened faith makes them see; for man cannot
persevere for long in what he does not love with his
whole heart.[94]

Charity itself is not always given in such a way that
the one who receives it takes in at once all that belongs
to its perfection. For charity is a love that can be overcome by another love, and often enough the love of
God is stifled by the love of the world; unless, kindled by
the Holy Spirit, it reaches such a state of fervour, that
no cold can extinguish it nor any tepidity slacken its ardour. Indeed, since the sum total of all God's bounty
and the soul of all virtues is given with this ineffable
gift, all other gifts are granted us to enable the yearning
of the faithful soul to strive effectively after perfect charity. As this is not only from God but is God Himself,[95]
it makes steadfast, persevering, and unconquerable all
those whom it floods with its delight. But men who do
not know the sweetness of these waters and still drink
of the torrents of this world; men who even after touching with the lips and tasting of the fountain of life, still

like to get drunk with the golden cup of Babylon,[96] are completely deceived by their own judgment and fall through their own fault. If they persist in this slothfulness, they themselves throw off what they had received. For without charity it is easy to lose all gifts, which same gifts are useless without charity.[97]

## CHAPTER 12

*When we turn away from God, this is our doing, not His ordinance. Man merits by persevering, because he could fall away.*

Let this brief survey of facts serve as a sure proof that God never forsakes any of the faithful who do not first turn away from Him,[98] and that His ordinance never plans any one's fall. Rather, many who have attained the use of reason are left capable of turning away from Him that they may be rewarded for not having done so, and that the merit of a behaviour which is not possible without the help of the Spirit of God, may yet belong to man by whose will it could have been absent. This will is by itself able to sin, but cannot by itself perform good works.[100] Though true virtue is in conformity with his nature, still the viciousness that has infected his nature following his evil will,[101] cannot be overcome by the power of nature but only by grace.

## CHAPTER 13

*Before the Flood God's goodness assisted with His
directions not only the saints but sinners also.*

The Spirit of God guided the first people of God,[102]
and thanks to the guidance of the Holy Spirit it kept
away from the intercourse and the ways of the cursed
and reprobate [103] people. Thus it preserved itself apart and
free from mixing with carnal men—men with whose evil
deeds God's patience bore up as long as good men could
please Him by not imitating them. But when the good
also became corrupted and imitated the wicked, and
when all mankind in wilful defection from God fell into
the same sinfulness, then one divine sentence destroyed
all, as all had fallen into the same ungodliness, except
only the house of Noe.

But God's goodness had not been withheld even from
the men who did not persevere in charity and who from
the beginning of their history were intoxicated with the
poison of a devilish envy. When the prince of the wicked
race, jealous of his saintly brother's merits and with frat-
ricide in his heart, was planning his murder, the Lord
deigned to soothe him with fatherly advice; He said to
Cain: *Why hast thou become gloomy? Why is thy
countenance fallen? Didst not thou, when thou didst
offer rightly but didst not divide rightly, incur sin? Calm
down. To thee will be the return therefrom, and thou
shalt have dominion over it.*[104] "Lay down," He says,
"thy sadness born from ill will and jealousy, and ex-

tinguish the flames of thy cruel hatred. Abel did not do thee any harm; by pleasing me he did not hurt thee. I despised thy offerings on my own judgment, not at his wish. For thou didst a good work negligently. Thy oblation would have been acceptable if thy discernment had been right. Knowing to whom thou wert offering, thou shouldst have known what to dedicate. Thou didst not make a worthy division between me and thyself because thou didst reserve for thyself the better things. That was thy mistake and thy sin. Calm down and do not be agitated against thy innocent brother. Let rather thy guilt come back on thee. Do not allow sin to reign in thee, but thou thyself rather take command over it.[105] Through repentance thou wilt both not fall into a greater sin and be cleansed from the one by which thou art sorry for having offended me."

When, therefore, we hear God speaking in this strain to Cain, can we have any doubt that He wished and—as much as was necessary for his conversion [106]—worked to bring him back to his senses from that frenzy of impiety? But Cain's obstinate malice became more inexcusable through what should have been its remedy. And, of course, God foreknew to what extremes his madness would drive him; yet, because of this infallible knowledge of God we may not conclude that his criminal will was urged on by any necessity to sin.[107] Truly, God could have saved Abel and kept him uninjured and untouched by Cain's murderous intention and action. But He was pleased to allow for the greater glory of His forbearance that the momentary frenzy of a wicked man should become the eternal glory of a just one.

As for the posterity of the parricide, who will not

easily see that God's goodness was not withheld from them, even though they lived in the same wicked way as their forebear? We must but consider what such a persevering patience of God, such rich abundance of temporal goods, and such numerous descendants due to their great fecundity could have meant to them.[108] Though these divine mercies did not bring any remedy or amendment of these obdurate sinners, they show, nevertheless, that their estrangement was not the effect of a divine ordinance but of their own wills.

CHAPTER 14

*At the time of the Flood and afterwards till the coming of Christ there were signs of the working of God's grace and figures of the miracles of Christian grace, although the abundant grace which now floods mankind did not then flow with such bounty.*

In the preservation of Noe with his sons and their wives,[109] who were to be the nursery of all the nations, Holy Scripture shows us the revelation of the wonders of divine grace. The ark of astounding capacity, which sheltered as many animals of all species as would be needed for the restoration of their kind, is the figure of the Church which is to assemble into herself the whole of mankind. In the wood and the water we see disclosed the Redemption through the Cross of Christ and the laver of regeneration. Those who were saved from the world-wide destruction symbolize the chosen fulness of all nations.[110] In them the gift of fecundity is renewed and the freedom to eat what they please is broadened, excluding only strangled things and blood;[111] and in the token of a many-coloured rainbow, that is, the symbol of God's multiform grace, solemn pledge of salvation is given.[112] All these mysteries and sacred signs[112a] were a teaching not only for the few members of one single family but also through them for all their posterity. The lesson God taught the parents was also meant for the instruction of their children.

Again, when the increase of the human race followed its upward course and men grew proud of their very numbers, and when their insolence rose to such a height that they dreamt of pushing up into heaven the massive structure of a building of fantastic proportions,[113] how wonderful was then the stricture of God's justice to stop their insolence! The one common language which all these people spoke and understood He threw into confusion and split it up into seventy-two tongues,[114] so as to break up by the confusion of their speech the unity of the workers and thus to foil the contrivance of their mad undertaking. At the same time God intended with the opportune dispersion of a union that had grown evil, to provide a population for the still uninhabited world. But in this work of God's Providence we also see prefigured the wonders of Christian grace which was to gather this entire dispersed humanity within the walls of that building where *every knee bows* to God *and every tongue confesses that Jesus is in the glory of the Father.*[115]

This diffusion of grace which was to be revealed in the

fulness of the appointed time, appears with still clearer signs in God's promise to Abraham, when He foretold him that his twofold posterity, that is, the children of the flesh and the children of the promise, would grow as numerous as the sand and the stars.[116] Then this old man, who by reason of the barrenness of his wife for years had already given up the hope of a son, believed with a faith that deserves praise, that through a single son he would become the father of the world. He foresaw, indeed, saw among his posterity Him who said, *Abraham saw my day and was glad.*[117]

At the time Abraham was justified through this faith, he had not yet received God's command about the circumcision; and though he was then in his natural uncircumcision, his faith was reputed to justice.[118] That same faith received the sign of the circumcision in the part of the body through which the seed of procreation was to advance to that flesh of which, without the seed of the flesh, the Son of God, God *the Word, was made flesh* [119] and was born of Abraham's daughter, the Virgin Mary. By His birth among men He made all men His brothers, who would be reborn in Christ through the Spirit and would have Abraham's faith. But up to the day that the seed should come of which it had been said, *In thy seed all the nations of the earth shall be blessed,*[120] this faith remained confined to the people of one race, and there with the true Israelites the hope of our Redemption was kept alive. For although there were some men of other races whom, whilst the Law was in force, the truth deigned to enlighten, yet they were so few that we can hardly know whether there were any.[121] But notwithstanding the fact that the abundance of grace which now

floods the whole world did not then flow with equal
bounty, this does not excuse the Gentiles who, *being
aliens from the conversation of Israel, . . . having no
hope, . . . and without God in this world,*[122] have died in
the darkness of their ignorance.

CHAPTER 15

*Men are not born now with a better nature than
before Christ; rather, at the time of His coming
the iniquity then existing was the more
pronounced in order the better to manifest the power of God's grace.*

God's revelation [123] was always imparted to all men in
some measure which, even when given more sparingly
and hiddenly, was yet judged sufficient by the Lord to
be a saving remedy for some and a testimony unto all.
Thus He made it clear beyond doubt that, if *where sin
abounded, grace had not abounded more,*[124] even now all
mankind would still be blinded by the same irreligion. Or,
to quote the nonsense spoken by many,[125] are men born
in our times better disposed than those of old? Have
these last ages produced souls that are more fit to receive
the divine gifts? Even if it were so, we would have to
attribute this to the goodness of their Maker who would
for the peoples whom He called to eternal life have fashioned hearts that would not resist Him. But it is not so.
There is nothing novel in the propagation of men according to the flesh. The younger generation is not born

superior to its forefathers. On the contrary, observation shows that regarding the men who lived when the Redeemer of the world came, the more recent the generation was, the greater was their iniquity.[126]

The proof of this is the impious frenzy of the Jews. The proof of how ready for the Gospel of Christ that generation was,[127] are the dispositions not only of the people but also of the scribes, the princes, and the priests. It was not enough for them, in opposition to the teaching of the Law, to the oracles of the Prophets, and to the proofs given them of divine power, to have vented their fury against *the Lamb of God that taketh away the sins of the world,*[128] in sedition, contumelies, spitting, buffets, blows, stoning, scourging, and, finally, the cruel death of the Cross. In their unchanged insanity they were to persecute also the witnesses of the Resurrection. But when scourged by the high priests, the Apostles showed how this had been foretold in the Psalm of David, saying: *Lord, Thou art He that didst make heaven and earth, the sea and all things that are in them. Who, by the Holy Spirit, by the mouth of our father David, Thy servant, hast said: "Why did the Gentiles rage and the people meditate vain things? The kings of the earth stood up, and the princes assembled together against the Lord and His Christ."* [129] *For of a truth there assembled together in this city against Thy holy Son Jesus, whom Thou hast anointed, Herod and Pontius Pilate, with the Gentiles and the people of Israel, to do what Thy hand and counsel decreed to be done.*[130]

Consequently, the reason why God withheld from the former ages the manifestation of the grace which in His eternal design He had prepared for the salvation of all

nations, is not that they were unfit for it. He rather
chose the times which produced such people as would, in
their wild and wilful malice, and not because they wished
to be helpful but because they intended to do harm, persist in carrying out the very counsels of God's hands.[131]
Thus God's grace and power would appear the more marvellous when He transformed these hardened souls, these
dark minds, these hostile hearts into His own people—
faithful, submissive, holy; who were led to the light of
God's wisdom not by the wisdom of this world, but
through the gift of Him to whom the Apostle John bears
witness in these words: *We know that the Son of God is
come. And He hath given us understanding that we may
know the true God and may be in His true Son.*[132] With
this testimony the Apostle Paul agrees when he says:
*Giving thanks to the Father who hath made us worthy
to be partakers of the lot of the saints in light; who hath
delivered us from darkness and from the power of darkness and hath translated us into the kingdom of the Son
of His love.*[133] And he again says: *For we . . . were some
time unwise, incredulous, erring, slaves to divers desires
and pleasures, living in malice and envy, hateful and
hating one another. But when the goodness and kindness
of . . . our Saviour appeared: not by works of justice
which we have done, but according to His mercy, He
saved us, by the laver of regeneration . . . of the Holy Spirit.
Whom He poured forth upon us abundantly, through
Jesus Christ our Saviour; that, being justified by His
grace, we may be heirs according to the hope of life everlasting.*[134]

Could he have explained more fully, more clearly, more
truly, what kind of merits Christ found in men, what

sort of characters He subjected to Himself, what kind of hearts He converted to Himself, when He came to heal, not the healthy, but the diseased, and to call, not the just, but sinners? [135] For *The people* of the Gentiles *that sat in darkness have seen a great light; and to them that sat in darkness and in the shadow of death, light is risen.*[136] The Gentiles howled, the peoples were angry, the kings raged, those in power spoke in opposition, the superstitions and errors of the whole world offered resistance. But from among those who resisted, who were enraged, and who persecuted, Christ chose to increase His people; and with the chains, tortures, and deaths of His saints the faith grew stronger, the truth conquered, and the wealth of the Lord's harvest spread throughout the whole world. Heaven gave so great a steadfastness in the faith, so great a trust in hope, so great a fortitude in endurance, that the fire of love kindled in the hearts of the faithful by the Holy Spirit could in no way be extinguished by their persecutors. Rather, those who were being tortured, were the more vehemently set on fire with love, and frequently their persecutors themselves were caught by the flame they were fighting.

Saint Paul the Apostle was on fire with that flame when, filled with trust and fervour, he said: *Being justified therefore by faith, let us have peace with God, through our Lord Jesus Christ; by whom also we have access through faith into grace wherein we stand, and glory in the hope of the glory of the sons of God. And not only so; but we glory also in tribulations, knowing that tribulation worketh patience; and patience trial; and trial hope; and hope confoundeth not, because the charity of God is poured forth in our hearts by the Holy Spirit who is given to us.*[137] And again: *Who . . . shall separate us from the love of Christ? Shall tribulation? Or distress? Or persecution? Or famine? Or nakedness? Or danger? Or the sword? (As it is written: "For Thy sake are we put to death all the day long. We are accounted as sheep for the slaughter.")* [138] *But in all these things we overcome through Him that hath loved us. For I am sure that neither death, nor life, nor angels, nor principalities, nor powers, nor things present, nor things to come, nor might, nor height, nor depth, nor any other creature shall be able to separate us from the love of God which is in Christ Jesus our Lord.*[139] With this charity diffused in their hearts by the Holy Spirit, the world of the faithful overcame the world of the unbelievers. This charity put to shame the cruelty of Nero, the fury of Domitian, and the frenzied rage of numerous emperors after them, in the glorious death of countless martyrs. There Christ bestowed on His followers through the persecution of the rulers the wreaths of their eternal crowns.

CHAPTER 16

*Christ died for all sinners.*

There can, therefore, be no reason to doubt that Jesus Christ our Lord died for the unbelievers and the sinners.[140] If there had been any one who did not belong to these, then Christ would not have died for all. But He did die for all men without exception. There is no one, therefore, in all mankind who was not, before the reconciliation which Christ effected in His blood, either a sinner or an unbeliever. The Apostle says: *For why did Christ, when as yet we were weak, according to the time, die for the ungodly? For scarce for a just man will one die; yet perhaps for a good man one would dare to die. But God commendeth His charity towards us, because if when as yet we were sinners, Christ died for us, much more, being justified by His blood, shall we be saved from wrath through Him. For if, when we were enemies, we were reconciled to God by the death of His Son, much more, being reconciled, shall we be saved by His life.*[141] The same Apostle says in his Second Epistle to the Corinthians: *For the charity of Christ presseth us, judging this, that if One died for all, then all were dead. And He died for all, that they also who live, may not live to themselves, but unto Him who died for them and rose again.*[142] And let us hear what he says of himself. *A faithful saying,* he states, *and worthy of all acceptation: that Christ Jesus came into this world to save sinners, of whom I am the chief. But for this cause have I obtained mercy: that in me first Christ Jesus might show forth all patience, for the information of them that shall believe in Him unto life everlasting.*[143]

Wherefore, the whole of mankind, whether circumcised or not, was under the sway of sin, in fetters because of the very same guilt. No one of the ungodly, who differed only in their degree of unbelief, could be saved without Christ's Redemption. This Redemption spread throughout the world to become the good news for all men without any distinction. In fact, on the fiftieth day after the paschal feast on which the true Lamb had offered Himself as a victim to God, when the Apostles and

those who were of one mind with them were filled with
the Holy Spirit and spoke the languages of all the nations,
a multitude of people of different races, stirred by the
miracle, flocked together, and in them the whole world
was to hear the Gospel of Christ. There were then assembled, as Scripture says, *Parthians, and Medes, and
Elamites, and inhabitants of Mesopotamia, Judea, and
Cappadocia, Pontus and Asia, Phrygia and Pamphylia,
Egypt and the parts of Lybia about Cyrene, and strangers
of Rome, Jews also and proselytes, Cretes and Arabians,*[144]
who all heard the wonderful works of God preached in
their own tongues. Their testimony was to spread far
and wide also to the more distant nations. We believe
that God's Providence had willed the expansion of the
Roman Empire as a preparation for His design over the
nations, who were to be called into the unity of the Body
of Christ: He first gathered them under the authority of
one empire.[145]

But the grace of Christianity is not content with the
boundaries that are Rome's. Grace has now submitted
to the sceptre of the Cross of Christ many peoples whom
Rome could not subject with her arms; though Rome
by her primacy of the apostolic priesthood has become
greater as the citadel of religion than as the seat of
power.[146]

## CHAPTER 17

*The nations that have not yet seen the grace
of our Saviour will be called to the
Gospel at the appointed time.*

It may be true that, just as we know that in former
times some peoples were not admitted to the fellowship
of the sons of God,[147] so also to-day there are in the remo-
test parts of the world some nations who have not yet
seen the light of the grace of the Saviour.[148] But we have
no doubt that in God's hidden judgment, for them also
a time of calling has been appointed, when they will hear
and accept the Gospel which now remains unknown to
them.[149] Even now they receive that measure of general
help which heaven [150] has always bestowed on all men.[151]
Human nature, it is true, has been wounded by such a
severe wound that natural speculation cannot lead a person to the full knowledge of God if the true light does not
dispel all darkness from his heart.[152] In His inscrutable
designs the good and just God did not shed this light
as abundantly in the past ages as He does in our own
day. That is why the blessed Apostle Paul says in writing to the Colossians: *The mystery which hath been hidden from ages and generations, but now is manifested in
His saints, to whom God would make known the riches
of the glory of this mystery among the Gentiles, which
is Christ in you.*[153]

CHAPTER 18

*In former ages the mystery of their call to the faith*
*was hidden from the Gentiles, but*
*not from the Prophets.*

Did this mystery also remain sealed for the Prophets?
Were they, the mouthpieces of the Holy Spirit, unaware
of what they were preaching? I do not think we have to
understand the text in that way, but only in the sense
that to the Gentiles this mystery [154] remained hidden—
a mystery which the Lord revealed when it pleased Him
and to whomsoever He pleased. For concerning the call
of the Gentiles, who did not belong to the people of God
and on whom at first God did not have mercy while now
He has shown mercy, we read in Deuteronomy as follows: *And the Lord saw and was roused and moved to*
*wrath because of the provocation of His sons and daugh-*
*ters. And He said: I will turn away my face from them,*
*and will show what will happen in the end. For it is a*
*perverse generation, children in whom there is no faith.*
*They have provoked me to anger with that which is no*
*god, they have angered me with their idols. And I will*
*provoke them to anger with them who were not a nation,*
*and I will vex them with a foolish nation.*[155] And David
foretells that all nations will adore God, in these words,
*All the nations Thou hast made shall come and adore be-*
*fore Thee, O Lord, and they shall glorify Thy name.*[156]
And the same again, *And all kings of the earth shall adore*

*Him, all nations shall serve Him.*[157] And again, *In Him shall all the tribes of the earth be blessed, all nations shall magnify Him.*[158]

Isaias also makes similar pronouncements, saying: *For in the last days the mountain of the Lord shall be manifest and the house of God on the top of the mountains, and it shall be exalted above the hills; and all nations shall come unto it.*[159] And the same says again: *And the Lord of hosts shall make unto all the nations in this mountain that they will drink wine in gladness, that they will be anointed with ointments on this mountain. He shall give all this to the nations, for this is His counsel concerning all the nations.*[160] And again: *And the Lord will reveal His holy arm in the sight of all the Gentiles, and all the nations of the earth shall see the salvation that cometh from the Lord.*[161] And again, *Behold, strangers shall come to thee through me, and take refuge with thee.*[162] And further: *Nations that knew thee not, will call on thee; and the peoples that know thee not, will run to thee.*[163]

Osee also prophesies the same things and says: *And it shall be in the place where it was said to them: You are not my people; there they will be called sons of the living God. And the children of Juda and the children of Israel shall be gathered together.*[164] And again: *I will have mercy on the not-beloved one. And I will say to that which was not my people: Thou art my people; and they shall say: Thou art my God.*[165]

At the time of the Apostles the believers in Christ who were of the circumcision expressed the opinion that the Gentiles, whom they called the uncircumcision, could not share in the justifying effects of grace. The blessed

Apostle Peter explains that before God there is no discrimination between both peoples as long as both are gathered in the unity of one faith. He says: *And when I had begun to speak, the Holy Spirit fell upon them, as upon us also in the beginning. And I remembered the word of the Lord, how that He said, "John indeed baptized with water, but you shall be baptized in the Holy Spirit."* [166] *If then God gave them the same grace as to us also who have believed in the Lord Jesus Christ; who was I, that could withstand God? Having heard these things, they held their peace and glorified God saying: God then hath also to the Gentiles given repentance unto life.*[167] The Apostle James also says about the call of the Gentiles: *Men, brethren, hear me. Simon hath related how God first visited to take of the Gentiles a people to His name. And to this agree the words of the Prophets, as it is written: "After these things I will return and will rebuild the tabernacle of David which is fallen down. And the ruins thereof I will rebuild, and I will set it up, that the residue of men may seek after the Lord, and all nations upon whom my name is invoked, saith the Lord, who doth those things."* [168] *To the Lord was His own work known from the beginning of the world.*[169] Simeon, too, the one to whom the Holy Spirit had said *that he should not see death before he had seen the Christ of the Lord,*[170] proclaimed the salvation of all the Gentiles as being revealed in Christ, as follows: *Now Thou dost dismiss Thy servant, O Lord, according to Thy word in peace; because my eyes have seen Thy salvation, which Thou hast prepared before the face of all peoples: a light to the revelation of the Gentiles, and the glory of Thy people Israel.*[171]

## CHAPTER 19

*God's will to save all men is active in all ages.*

These [172] and other evidences from the Scriptures prove beyond doubt [173] that the great wealth, power, and beneficence of grace which in these last times [174] calls all the Gentiles into the kingdom of Christ, was in former centuries hidden in the secret counsel of God.[175] No knowledge can comprehend, no understanding can penetrate the reason why this abundance of grace which has now come to the knowledge of all nations, was not revealed to them before. Yet we believe with complete trust in God's goodness that *He wills all men to be saved and to come to the knowledge of the truth:* [176] this we must hold as His changeless will from eternity,[177] which manifests itself in the different measures in which He in His wisdom chose to augment His general gifts [178] with special favours. Thus those who did not share in His grace,[179] plead guilty of malice, and those who were resplendent with its light, cannot glory in their own merit but only in the Lord.

## CHAPTER 20

*Objection against the text, "who wills all men to be saved," taken from the case of infants.*

This subtle but correct way of understanding our problem is confronted by a great difficulty in the case of infants.[180] Infants have not the use of reason by which they can understand the mercies of their Maker and be enabled to approach to the knowledge of truth. It would not seem right to blame them for neglecting the help of grace, when they are by their nature in such a state of ignorance that they are unable—and there can be no doubt about it—to acquire any knowledge or to grasp any teaching. If, then, *God wills all men to be saved*,[181] what is the reason why so great a number of infants remain deprived of eternal salvation, and why so many thousands of human beings at this tender age are not admitted to eternal life? [182]

It would look as if God, who created no one out of hatred, had created these children only to throw them in the bonds of an unforgivable guilt which they contracted without any fault of their own, for the only reason that they entered this world in a flesh of sin.[183] What can be more unfathomable, more astounding than this? [184] For it would not be right to believe that these children who have not received the sacrament of regeneration, do in any way belong to the communion of the Blessed.[185] And what makes it still more stupendous and strange is this: here we have no guilt incurred through actions, no free wills capable of offering resistance; there is misfortune which is the same for all, there is equal helplessness—a case precisely the same for all. Yet, in spite of this complete parity of their case, the judgment is not the same for all; but [186] some He disowns as reprobate, others He adopts as His elect.[187]

CHAPTER 21

*God is just when He rejects unbaptized infants both in this life and in the next because of original sin.*

But if we are humble of heart we shall not be disturbed by the unfathomable depth of this discrimination of God.[188] We must but believe with firm and steadfast faith that all of God's judgments are just,[189] and not wish to know what He wanted to remain secret. Where we cannot possibly investigate the reason of His judgment, we should rest content with knowing who He is that judges.[190] Though our problem is not so obscure that we can learn from it nothing whatever. We must only with the peaceful gaze of a discreet mind consider what we are able to know.

For instance, let us reflect on this. Among pagans, among Jews, among heretics, and among Catholic Christians also, how large a number of children die who manifestly, as far as their own wills go, have done neither good nor evil! But we are told that on them weighs the sentence which the human race received for the sin of Adam, our first father. And the rigour of this sentence, which is not relaxed even for children, proves only how grave that sin was.[191] Were children not to suffer harm from their privation of baptism, then also [192] we would no longer believe that no one is born in innocence.

And there is no reason to complain that death comes too early for them, because once mortality invaded our nature through sin,[193] every day of our life was forfeited to it. There would be reason for complaint if there were a time when man could not die at all and he could thus be said to have a limited immortality. But at no moment does our corruptible nature share in incorruption to the extent that, when it is born for death, it would not always be liable to decay. The beginning of life is the commencement of death. No sooner do we advance in age than we start to decline. When a space of time is added to our age, this is not an addition resulting in a state of stability, but a mere form of transition to death. Therefore, if a being is perishable from its inception, whatever day it passes away, it does not perish contrary to the law of mortality. It is never so fully in possession of life that it is not within the grasp of death.[194] And, although the mortality of all mankind has sprung from one source, yet our corruptible nature is torn asunder not by one but by many kinds of weakness. Illness, debility, accidents threaten not only the years or months or days of our human existence but every hour and every minute. There is no kind of death, no manner of leaving this world which does not befall some portion of mortal mankind.[195] For there remains *a heavy yoke upon the children of Adam, from the day of their coming out of their mother's womb until the day of their burial into the mother of all.*[196]

## CHAPTER 22

*Divine justice measures out to each one his lot of misfortune.*

But the weight of this most heavy yoke [197] did not so fall on the sons of Adam that God's justice would in no way apply to it [198] His own standards. According to these He submitted defective beings to the laws of their deficiencies, but at the same time did not withhold from them His power of mitigating their miseries. [199] He did not allow that, just because all men on account of their common sinful condition are liable to all evils, each and every evil should befall each and every man. The Lord wished that general necessity to assert itself in varying degrees, while keeping to Himself the reasons both for indulgence and for severity; and the one debt common to all was to both make of His forgiveness a mercy and of His punishment an act of justice. [200]

We know, then, that God's just and omnipotent Providence governs all things unceasingly; that nobody comes into this world or departs from it except as the Lord of all things, in His unfathomable knowledge and wisdom, has decreed his birth or death; [201] as is written in the Book of Job: *Who is ignorant that the hand of the Lord hath made all these things? In whose hand is the soul of every living being, and the spirit of all flesh of man;* [202] and again, *The days of man are short, and the number of his days is with Thee.* [203] Who would dare search into the reasons of His works and counsels? For inscrutable and great is the secret reason why men, whose human condition is the same, are treated in so different ways. One is harassed from childhood to old age with a long illness, and in spite of persisting pains no moment is cut off from his appointed lifetime; while another enjoys the full strength of his powers with a vigorous health up to [204] an old age. To one death comes in childhood, to another in adolescence. One is not allowed to go beyond youth, another cannot even reach the age of speech. Our frail mortality would find all this delimitation of life, so unequal in many respects, less bitter if there were the loss of the present life only, and if children who depart from this world without the laver of regeneration did not fall into unending misery.[205]

CHAPTER 23

*Children who die receive the general grace
bestowed upon their parents.*

The reason that regulates the distribution of the gifts of grace is more inscrutable for us than the cause of the miseries which our nature deserved. But this very difficulty in understanding the mystery makes us look up to our Maker.[206] If we ask, how it can be said that *God wills all men to be saved,*[207] when He does not grant to all the time when they are able to receive grace in a free acceptance of the faith, I think we may believe without irreverence towards God and conceive without impropriety, that those human beings who live only a few days share in the kind of grace [208] which has always been given to all nations.

For indeed, if the parents were to make good use of this grace, the children also would derive a saving help from it through them.[209] In fact, all children depend for their birth and during the whole time of their infancy up to the age of reason on the decisions made by other men, and the guidance given them must come exclusively from others.[210] Thus it follows that infants share the lot of those persons whose right or wrong dispositions decide their condition.[211] Some of them happen to have the faith through the profession of faith of other people;[212] in the same way some fail to have the faith on account of the unbelief or the guilty neglect of others. Though they themselves had no desire either of the present life or of the future, yet, just as their birth has become their own concern, so also the eventual privation of rebirth becomes their own.[213] And just as in the case of adults it is obvious that some, in addition to the general grace which moves all human hearts in a more sparing and more hidden way, receive a special call—with more excellent effects of grace, with more generous gifts, and with a stronger power; so also in the case of the countless infants the same election reveals itself.[214] The election was not withheld even from the children who failed to receive baptism, when it was present in their parents; but it reached some children who were baptised, without reaching their parents.[215] Thus it often happened that children were taken care of by strangers when their unbelieving kinsfolk failed them; and through strangers they came to receive regeneration when their own people would not have provided this for them.[216]

CHAPTER 24

*We can find no reason for a just complaint in the different*
*destiny of children who in all other respects*
*are alike; rather there is a strong proof of*
*God's justice and of Christ's grace.*

In this economy of grace [217] who but one altogether
insolent and benighted could complain of divine justice,
because Providence does not treat all children in the same
way, and because its power does not discard, nor its
mercy forestall, all perils that may prevent the regeneration of such as are bound to die? This would indeed be
done for all children, if it had to be done by all means. [218]

But it is not difficult to see what carelessness would
arise in [219] the hearts of the faithful, if in the matter of
the baptism of children the neglect of a person or the possibility of their dying offered no cause for fear; for in that
hypothesis it could never happen that children would remain deprived of baptism. [220] But this supposition, that
the happiness of children can never be frustrated, would
add great strength to the erroneous opinion which ventures to say, in opposition to our Catholic faith, that men
receive grace according to their merit. [221] For then it would
look as though the guiltless innocence of infants could
claim in full justice that not one of their number should
fail to receive this adoption, because no guilt holds them
in chains. Then there would have been nothing against
the faith in the statement made by someone about the
baptism of children: "Grace has something to adopt, but

the water of baptism has nothing to cleanse." [222] But all followers of the truth see the execrable implication of the gospel preached here. It is obvious that all who die without baptism are lost; [223] and this fact proves by itself that all men who attain salvation owe this, not to their own merit, but to grace. Certainly, were not the others stained with a very grave sin, they would not be lost.[224] But as it is, God's discriminating judgment, hidden but just, manifests both the gift which grace bestows on man and the punishment which sinful nature deserves. Thus no human pride can boast that grace is not a gift, nor may our diligence relax as though there were no danger to fear.

CHAPTER 25

*With His general grace given to all, God always wills and has willed all men to be saved; but His special grace is not granted to all.*

Whether, then, we look on these last centuries or on the first or on the ages between, we see that reason and religious sense alike make us believe that God wills and has always willed all men to be saved.[225] We prove this from no other source than from the very gifts which God's Providence generally bestows on all men without any distinction. These gifts are found to be so general in the past and in the present, that men find in their testimony  sufficient help to seek the true God.[226] Over and above these gifts which proclaim their Maker throughout the ages, God has scattered a special bounty of grace.

And though this grace is bestowed more abundantly nowadays than before, yet the Lord has reserved to Himself the knowledge of the reasons of His dispensations and kept them hidden in the secrecy of His all-powerful will.[227] Were these to come to all men uniformly, then there would be nothing hidden about them.[228] And just as there can be no doubt about His general kindness to all men, so also there would be nothing astounding concerning His special mercy.[229] Consequently, the former would appear to be a grace, while the latter would not.[230] But God was pleased to grant this latter grace to many and to withhold the former from no one. He wished to make it clear from both that He did not refuse to all mankind what He gave to some men,[231] but that in some men grace prevailed and in others nature recoiled.[232]

CHAPTER 26

*In every justification grace is the outstanding factor, while the human will is a secondary one, united with grace and co-operating with God working in man; grace prepares the will for this co-operation.*[233]

We believe and we know from experience that this abundant grace acts in man as a powerful influence; but in our opinion this influence is not such as to be overpowering, to the extent that whatever transpires in men's salvation is achieved by God's will alone; [234] for already in the case of children it is the assent of another man's will that is the medium for them to be relieved of their affliction.[235] The special grace of God is certainly the more prominent factor in every justification. It urges on with exhortations, moves by examples, inspires fear from dangers, rouses with miracles, gives understanding, inspires counsel, illumines the heart itself and inspires it with the aspirations of the faith.[236]

But man's will is also associated with grace as a secondary factor. For it is roused by the above-mentioned aids in order that it may co-operate with God's work which is being accomplished in man, and that it may begin to practise and gain merit from that for which the divine seed inspires the effective desire.[237] Thus its eventual failure is due to its own fickleness; but its success is due to the help of grace.

This help is given in countless ways, some of which are hidden, and others are easily discernible. If many refuse this help, it is only their malice that is the cause. If many accept it, then this is due to both divine grace and their human will.[238] We may examine the beginning of faith in the faithful or their progress or final perseverance in it, nowhere shall we discover any sort or kind of virtue which it not the fact of both the gift of grace and the consent of our wills. For grace, in all the variety of remedy or help which it provides, first operates to prepare the will of the recipient of its call to accept and follow up its gifts. Virtue is non-existent with men who do not wish to be virtuous,[239] and you cannot say that men could have faith or hope or charity, if they refuse their free consent to these virtues.

CHAPTER 27

*Grace causes the consent of our will not only by teaching
and enlightening but also through terror and fear.*

Men give their free consent to grace not only when
induced to do so by the exhortation of preachers and the
inspiration of doctrine, but also through fear.[240] That is
why we read in the Scripture, *The fear of the Lord is the
beginning of wisdom.*[241] This fear, the result of frighten-
ing experiences of whatever sort, tends only to make a
man willing who began by fearing, and not only willing
but also wise. That is why Scripture says again, *Blessed
is the man to whom it is given to have the fear of God.*[242]
For what gives greater happiness than this fear which
produces and fosters wisdom? With the devotion that
springs from wisdom the will also is filled, and thanks to
the same fear which first stirred it to action and then
produced grace, the will now starts making progress.[243]
When this fear is struck into a man even with the shock
of a great fright, this does not mean that it blots out his
reason or deprives him of his understanding. It rather
dispels the darkness that oppressed the mind, so that his
will, which was before depraved and captive, is now set
right and free.[244] Consequently, just as the soul acquires
no virtue unless it has received a ray of the true light,[245]
so also grace bestows no favour on the man whom it
calls, unless it has first opened the eyes of his will.[246]

As was discussed above,[247] in many men grace produces
great fervour from its first stirrings and then it is quickly
enriched with considerable increase. But in many also

who advance slowly and hesitatingly, it hardly grows strong enough to reach the firmness that is necessary for perseverance. Our Lord indeed says, *No man can come to me, except the Father, who hath sent me, draw him.*[248] But Christ said this to teach us that faith, without which no one can come to Him, is a gift of the Father, as was shown in what He said to the Apostle Peter: *Blessed art thou, Simon Bar-Jona; because flesh and blood hath not revealed it to thee, but my Father who is in heaven.*[249] It is the Father who in the hearts of the men He wished to draw to Himself produced both the faith and the good will. For they could not have been so drawn had they not followed freely through faith and good will.[250] Men who refuse the faith are neither drawn to Him nor do they come to Him. When they withhold their free consent, they do not come nearer, they rather go farther away from Him. It is love that leads to Him all those who come to Him.[251] He loved them first and they returned His love. He sought them first and they in turn sought Him; and when God inspired their will with His own, they willingly followed Him.[252]

## CHAPTER 28

*The faithful who by God's grace believe in Christ remain free not to believe; and those who persevere may yet turn away from God.*

He who inspires men with the desire to obey Him, does not take away from them, even from those who will persevere, the fickleness by which they can still refuse obedience.[253] If it were otherwise, then none of the faithful would ever have given up the faith, concupiscence would overcome no one nor sadness depress any one; anger would vanquish no one and the charity of no one would grow cold; no one's patience would give way and no one would neglect the grace that is offered him. But since these things can take place and men all too easily and readily yield and consent to such temptations, the words which our Lord spoke to His Apostles, *Watch ye and pray that ye enter not into temptation,*[254] should ever keep ringing in the ears of the faithful. Had He admonished His disciples to watch only and not to pray also, then it might appear that He wished only to rouse the energy of their free wills. But by adding, *and pray,* He showed well enough that it would be thanks to a gift from heaven together with their watchfulness that they would stand firm in the storm of temptation.

In the same sense He said: *Simon, Simon, behold Satan hath desired to have you, that he may sift you as wheat. But I have prayed for thee, that thy faith fail not; and thou, being converted in the end, confirm thy brethren.*[255] *And pray lest ye enter into temptation.*[256] When the faith of so great an Apostle was going to give way unless Christ prayed for him,[257] this was a sure sign that he, too, was subject to unsteadiness which could falter in temptation; and he was not so confirmed with the strength to persevere, that he was not liable to any weakness. For indeed, even after all this, trepidation was to shake him so badly that in the house of Caiphas, frightened by the questions of some servant girl, his constancy was to give way, and that to the extent of disowning Christ [258] three times, after he had promised to die for Him. At that moment He looked on the troubled heart of His Apostle not with human but with divine eyes,[259] and with a piercing glance stirred it to abundant tears of repentance. The Lord could also have given the chief of His disciples such firmness of soul that, as He Himself was not to be deterred from the resolve to undergo His Passion, so Saint Peter also on that occasion would not have been overcome by any fear.

But such steadfastness belonged only to Him who alone could say in truth and reality, *I have power to lay down my life, and I have power to take it up again.*[260] In all other men, as long as *the flesh lusteth against the spirit, and the spirit against the flesh,*[261] and as long as *the spirit indeed is willing, but the flesh is weak,*[262] immovable strength of soul is not to be found, because the perfect and undisturbed happiness of peace is not our lot in this life, but in the next only. But in the uncertainty of the present struggle, when the whole of life is a trial [263] and when victory itself is not shielded from the Waylayer's pride, the danger of inconstancy is ever present. True, God's protection gives the strength of final perseverance to His countless saints, yet He does not free any of them from the resistance which their efforts encounter in their own nature. In all their exertions and endeavours the struggle between willingness and unwillingness continues unabated.[264]

The most blessed Peter himself passed through this conflict at the very moment when he was about to crown all his victories. That is what our Lord foretold him when He said: *Amen, amen, I say to thee, when thou wast younger, thou didst gird thyself and didst walk where thou wouldst. But when thou shalt be old, thou shalt stretch forth thy hands, and another shall gird thee and lead thee whither thou wouldst not. And this He said signifying by what death he should glorify God.*[265] Who, then, would doubt, who would fail to see that this strongest of rocks, who shared in the strength and the name of the first Rock,[266] had always nourished the wish to be given the strength of dying for Christ? Yet even he was not to escape the impact of terror. This man who was most anxious to suffer martyrdom heard the promise that he would indeed be victorious in his sufferings, but not without the test of fear.

Rightly, therefore, do not only beginners but advanced saints as well beseech the Lord in the same manner and say, *Lead us not into temptation, but deliver us from evil.*[267] For to all who persevere in faith and charity it is He who grants the strength not to be overcome in temptation, that *he that glorieth may glory in the Lord.*[268] And though it is He who gives them the victory,[269] He attributes to them the merit of it. Though it is only with God's help that they stood firm in temptation, yet because they were of their nature exposed to falling, He reckons it to their credit that they remained steadfast.[270] Consequently, just as those who are believers receive help to persevere in their faith, so they also who are still unbelievers receive help to come to the faith. And just as it is possible for the former to leave the faith, so are unbelievers capable not to come to it.[271] It is clear, then, that in a countless variety of ways *God wills all men to be saved and to come to the knowledge of the truth.*[272] When they do come, then God's help is their guide; and when they do not, the fault of the refusal lies with their own obstinacy.

CHAPTER 29

*God is fulfilling His promise to bless all the nations*
*every day, so as not to leave any excuse to*
*the reprobate, nor to give the elect a*
*reason to glory in their justice.*

Many people [273] are in love with their own darkness
and do not accept the splendour of the truth. Many who
have seen the light return to their darkness. Yet *the word*
*of God endureth for ever,*[274] and no tittle of His truthful
promise lacks fulfilment. Every day the foreknown and
promised fulness of the Gentiles [275] enters the fold, and
in the seed of Abraham every nation, every tribe, every
language receives His blessings.[276] For what the Father
gave to the Son, the Son does not lose,[277] and no one can
snatch from His hand what He has received.[278] *The sure*
*foundation of God standeth firm,*[279] and the building of
the temple that will stand forever does not shake, because God's truth and mercy cover all men. God effects
in the men who come within His promise what He refuses to no one and what He owes to no one.[280] He Himself *worketh all in all,*[281] and *all* that He works cannot but
be just and good.[282] For *all the ways of the Lord are justice*
*and truth.*[283]

God foreknew before all ages how many from all over
the world would, though they enjoyed His general gifts
or were even aided with His special helps,[284] still stray
from the path of truth and life and take the broad road
of error and death. He likewise ever saw in His prescience

how many God-fearing men, thanks to the help of His grace and to their own obedient service, would enter into eternal beatitude.[285] Thus, while no one was to fall from the number of the promised elect, except those who would fail to make progress or would neglect to profit by His help, He was to exalt in glory above all the elect whom He chose from all mankind. Certainly, as we have proved abundantly, God's manifold and ineffable goodness always provided and still provides for all mankind [286] in such a way that not one of the reprobate can find an excuse as though he had been refused the light of truth, and that no one can rightly boast of his own justice. The one group perishes by reason of its own malice,[287] while it is God's grace that leads the other into glory.

CHAPTER 30

*Recapitulation of chapter one, Book Two.*

We wish to recommend here again what we had suggested at the beginning of this Second Book, namely, that when we treat about the depth and height of divine grace, we should base our reasoning on these three propositions which are perfectly sound and true. One of these declares that God's goodness from all eternity and of His own free choice wills all men *to be saved and to come to the knowledge of the truth.*[288] With this goes another, stating that every man who is actually saved and comes to the knowledge of the truth, owes it to God's help and guidance just as he owes to Him his perseverance in faith *that worketh by charity.*[289] A third acknowledges with modesty and circumspection that we cannot comprehend the motive of every divine decree and that the reasons of many of God's works remain hidden from our human understanding.[290]  We see that God acts in a different or even in a singular way at different times, when dealing with different nations or families, with infants or the unborn, or even with twins.[291] We have no doubt that here we are facing those things which God in His justice and mercy does not wish us to know in this fleeting world.

And we must be persuaded that this was thus disposed for our good.  Thus, seeing that *we are saved by hope* [292] and that God has prepared for us *that eye hath not seen, nor ear heard neither hath it entered into the heart of man;* [293] and just as we firmly believe that some day we shall see what we do not yet see, so also we wait patiently to understand what we do not yet understand. Wherefore, if all spite and subtlety are put aside and if all insolent presumption bows down, then, after all that we have said, and said correctly, I think, there will be no matter left for further quarrel, and there will be no further need for us to busy ourselves with endless discussions.

CHAPTER 31

*In all ages God's general goodness gave grace to all men, but to the elect He gave His special grace.*

We have endeavoured to prove as best we could with the Lord's help,[294] that not only in our own day but in all past ages as well God gave His grace to all men, provid-

ing equally for all and showing to all His general goodness, yet in such a manner that the effects of His grace
are manifold and the measure of His gifts varying. For
in hidden or open ways He is, as the Apostle says, *the
Saviour of all men, especially of the faithful*.[295] This statement is subtle in its brevity [296] and strong in its conclu-
siveness. If we consider it with a calm mind, we shall
notice that it decides the whole of the present controversy.
For by saying, *who is the Saviour of all men*, the Apostle
affirmed that God's goodness is general and takes care of
all men. But by adding, *especially of the faithful*, he
showed that there is a section of humankind whom God,
thanks to their faith which He himself inspired, leads on
with special helps to the supreme and eternal salvation.[297]
In doing this, God, who is supremely just and merciful,
is above all injustice, and we have not to discuss His
judgment about these rulings—that would be arrogance—
but rather to praise it in awe and trembling.

CHAPTER 32

*Among the faithful there are different degrees in God's
gifts, and this is not due to their merit but
to God's just and hidden judgment.*

In fact, among the faithful themselves, as we have already shown above,[298] these gifts are not the same and are
not equal for all. Before human merit can have any influence, the divine mercies are measured out most unequally. Rightly so. If we dare not complain of the

decision of human parents when they show more indulgence and love for some of their children even before they have considered their behaviour or received from them any filial services; if we allow human masters also the free disposal of their servants, and if we cannot justly censure one who in a household of the same social standing chooses those to whom he wishes to give greater privileges and to provide with a more liberal education: [299] must we then find fault with the most benevolent justice of the supreme Father and the true Master, because in His large household He disposes all things in countless ways and variations? Though no man has any good which he was not given by God, yet not all are resplendent with the same virtues or endowed with the same gratuitous gifts. And we may not see the reason of these different degrees in their different merits; it is rather grace which is the first cause of all merit, and which produces all that is praiseworthy in each and every one.[300]

## CHAPTER 33

*Not one of the elect is lost, but all who were chosen from all eternity attain salvation.*

Therefore,[301] just as our religious sense forbids us to harbour in our hearts any complaint about the multifarious operations of the Holy Spirit within the Church,[302] in the same manner we should in no way murmur about God's Providence which rules the destiny of the infidels. For our Master who is both just and kind, cannot will anything unjust nor waver in His discernment. We must, then, not fancy that, in spite of the immeasurable mercy and justice of almighty God, a man who is not a reprobate would be lost.[303]

No part of the world is left without the Gospel of Christ.[304] And although that general call of His does not cease, yet the special call [305] has now also reached the whole of mankind. From every nation and every condition thousands of aged people, thousands of youths, thousands of children daily receive the grace of adoption. The very armies that exhaust the world help on the work of Christian grace. How many indeed who in the quiet of peace-time delayed to receive the sacrament of baptism, were compelled by fear of close danger to hasten to the water of regeneration, and were suddenly forced by threatening terror to fulfil a duty which a peaceful exhortation failed to bring home to their slow and tepid souls? Some sons of the Church, made prisoners by the enemy, changed their masters into servants of the Gospel, and by teaching them the faith they became the superiors of their own wartime lords. Again, some foreign pagans, whilst serving in the Roman armies, were able to learn the faith in our country,[306] when in their own lands they could not have known it; they returned to their homes instructed in the Christian religion. Thus nothing can prevent God's grace from accomplishing His will. He makes even of dissensions a bond of union and turns misfortunes into remedies. Thus where the Church feared danger, there she finds her expansion.[307]

Consequently, to whatever course of human events we direct our attention, we shall find out that no centuries or events, no rising or falling generations are independent of God's eternal and inscrutable judgments. All conflicts of opposed interests and all the causes of confusing events [308] which we are not able to search into and to explain, are simultaneously known and clear to God's eternal knowledge. There nothing is unsettled even of the modalities of actions that are still to come. For in God there is neither sudden impulse, nor new will, nor temporary design. His thought does not alter with the alternations of changeable things, but He comprehends with His eternal and immovable glance all times and things of time alike. He has already rendered all to all, since He has already accomplished what is still to come. [309]

Hence the well-known text of the blessed Apostle Paul to the Ephesians: *Blessed be the God and Father of our Lord Jesus Christ, who hath blessed us with spiritual blessings in heavenly places, in Christ, as He chose us in Him before the foundation of the world, that we should be holy and unspotted in His sight in charity. Who hath predestined us unto the adoption of children through Jesus Christ in Himself, according to the purpose of His will, unto the praise of the glory of His grace,*[310] and so the rest of the text where the Apostle expresses the same idea. He teaches that the gift and the effect of grace always existed in God's eternal design, and that God chose all His sons of adoption not only when He called them during their lifetime, but before the world was established. No one of mankind who was not foreknown as an elect in Christ, will in any way share in the election.[311] For all who at any time will be called and will enter into the kingdom of God, have been marked out in the adoption which preceded all times.[312] And just as none of the infidels is counted among the elect, so none of the God-fearing is excluded from the blessed. For in fact God's prescience which is infallible, cannot lose any of the members that make up the fulness of the Body of Christ. And the number of the elect who were foreknown and fore-chosen in Christ before all times, can in no way be diminished; [313] as the Apostle writes to Timothy: *Labour with the gospel, according to the power of God, who hath delivered us and called us by a holy calling, not according to our works, but according to His own purpose and grace, which was given us in Christ Jesus before time eternal.*[314]

CHAPTER 34

*Though God's design about the salvation of the elect is without change, yet it is not useless to work and to acquire the merit of good actions, and also to keep on praying.*

To this blinding light of the invincible truth some people are wont to object unwisely: If the election of the grace of Christianity is fixed already in God's changeless counsel, and if nothing can turn out otherwise than was settled by the will of the Almighty, then it is superfluous to labour and to acquire the merit of good works, and it is useless to go on with prayers by which we hope to prevail upon Him.[315] But if they fancy that their objection is an acute one, then they fail to see that God's knowledge which embraces the past, the present, and the future, is not encompassed by time, and that future events are as present to Him as are current or past ones. Since this is absolutely true, this power which sees at a glance that is everlasting and truthful both what was created and is still to be, what was born and will be born, what was done and is still to be done, is not in need of time to look and discern. All that comes to pass in the whole universe through the appointed ages and is unrolled in a multitude of various events, it comprehends now in its entirety, in the same order in which till the end of the world it will take place according to His supreme and perfect judgment.[316]

But this eternal and ever serene knowledge does not impose on us any necessity of sinning,[317] and no iniquity can spring from the source of all justice. For, since the good God made all things good, and evil has no nature of its own at all,[318] it is from free wills that a wilful transgression arose; yet it was good that these wills were created free. Our fickle nature whose integrity depended on the changeless Essence, tore itself away from the supreme Good when taking pleasure in that which was its own.[319] It is for this fall that God's grace now brings the remedy.

CHAPTER 35

*The elect receive grace, not to allow them to be idle or to free them from the Enemy's attacks, but to enable them to work well and to conquer the Enemy.*

And for that reason[320] Jesus Christ came into this world, *that He might destroy the works of the devil.*[321] He effects this destruction in such a manner that the men whom He helps have an active part in it, and this also is a gift of the Saviour. That is why the blessed Apostle says: *And not only so: but we glory also in tribulations, knowing that tribulation worketh patience; and patience trial; and trial hope; and hope confoundeth not; because the charity of God is poured forth in our hearts by the Holy Spirit who is given to us.*[322] In like manner he says to the Ephesians: *By grace you are saved through faith and that not of yourselves, for it is a gift of God; not of works, that no man may glory. For we are His handiwork, created in Christ . . . in good works, which God hath prepared that we should walk in them.*[323]

God, then, grants to His elect whom He chose without any merit of their own, the means to gain merit.[324] And in vain would you say that the elect have no reason to labour; they were rather chosen that they should labour.[325] For God's gifts, which are the virtues, cannot remain idle, because, as the Truth says, *To every one that hath shall be given, . . . but from him that hath not, that also which he hath shall be taken away.*[326] Consequently, God does not give continence to allow a man not to resist his inordinate desires. He does not give wisdom and understanding to dispense a man from meditating on the Lord's law day and night.[327] What can the gift of charity effect if a man is not ever animated by a desire to help others? What can be the fruit of patience if fortitude has no chance to suffer? Or how will a man give proof that the life he lives is really devoted to Christ,[328] if he does not suffer any persecution? Or does the peace a man enjoys from God and with God, give the right sort of quiet if it is not in opposition to the world? Or can a man have the friendship of God without enmity of the devil? God's grace does not make any one proof against temptation.

The Christian soldier is not equipped with heavenly weapons, both offensive and defensive, in order not to fight with any enemy; because it brings greater glory and happiness to come through battle invincible than to prove unassailable because of indolence.

CHAPTER 36

*Election does not dispense from application to prayer,*
*rather it reaches its fulfilment through the*
*medium of prayer and good works.*

That the design of the divine election does not do away with attention to prayer,[329] I shall prove with evidence from one text, omitting all others for the sake of briefness. In the Book of Tobias the angel Raphael says to Tobias, the son: *Remember the commandments of thy father, that he ordered thee to take a wife*[330] *from the family of thy father. And now, hear me, brother, do not take into account that devil; but ask for her. And know that she will be given thee for wife this night. And when thou shalt enter into the chamber, take of the liver of that fish, and put it on the coals: a smell will spread, and the devil shall smell it, and he will be driven away, and he shall never anymore make his appearance about her. And when thou shalt begin to desire to be with her, first rise both, and pray the Lord of heaven, that mercy and health be given you. And do not fear, for she was destined for thee before the centuries, and thou shalt heal her.*[331]

Therefore, although it is impossible that God's decree

would not come true, yet it does not do away with the practice of prayer, nor does the design of the election diminish the effort of man's free will. God rather preordained the effect He intended in such a way that He desires man's merit to grow through the labour of good works, through perseverance in supplications, through the practice of virtues. He wants to crown the good works of men not only according to His own plan but also according to their merits. And clearly it is for this reason that He hides the preordination of their election in a secrecy quite inaccessible to human knowledge.[332]

## CHAPTER 37

*Of no man can it be stated before his death that he will share the glory of the elect; on the other hand, there is no reason to despair of any fallen man's conversion.*

And of no man can the verdict be given before his death that he will share in the glory of the elect; rather, a salutary fear should make him persevere in humility. *Let him that standeth, take heed lest he fall;* [333] and if he should happen to fall, overcome by a temptation, let him not be consumed by sadness, nor despair of the mercy of Him *who lifteth up all that fall, and setteth up all that are cast down.* [334] For as long as we live in our bodies we must not neglect to correct any one, nor despair of any one's conversion.[335]

Let, then, Holy Church pray, let her give thanks for

those who have received the faith, let her make entreaty for their progress and perseverance. Let her plead on behalf of infidels that they may believe.[336] And when her prayers are not heard for some of them, let her not desist from praying. For God who *wills all men to come to the knowledge of the truth*,[337] cannot repel any one without a just reason.

# NOTES

# LIST OF ABBREVIATIONS

| | |
|---|---|
| ACW | Ancient Christian Writers |
| B | Ballerini text of *De vocatione* |
| CSEL | Corpus scriptorum ecclesiasticorum latinorum |
| DAFC | Dictionnaire apologétique de la foi catholique, 4th ed., ed. by A. d'Alès |
| DSAM | Dictionnaire de spiritualité ascétique et mystique |
| DTC | Dictionnaire de théologie catholique |
| ES | Enchiridion symbolorum, 21st ed., ed. by H. Denziger, C. Bannwart, J. B. Umberg |
| Hefele-Leclercq | Histoire des conciles |
| M | Mangeant text of *De vocatione* |
| Mansi | Sacrorum conciliorum nova et amplissima collectio |
| ML | P. J. Migne, Patrologia latina |
| TLL | Thesaurus linguae latinae |

# INTRODUCTION

[1] The title of the treatise reads *Duo libri de vocatione omnium gentium*, meaning two books intended to prove that all nations are the object of God's call to salvation. *Omnium gentium* reflects, no doubt, a term occurring frequently in the New Testament: e.g. Matt. 24. 14 ('in testimonium *omnibus gentibus*'); 28. 19 ('docete *omnes gentes*'); Mark 13. 10 ('in *omnes gentes* . . . oportet praedicari Evangelium'); Luke 24. 47; etc.

[2] For the latest study on Pelagius, cf. G. de Plinval, *Pélage, ses écrits, sa vie et sa réforme* (Lausanne 1943); for the history of Pelagianism and Semi-Pelagianism, the chapters, 'Les luttes pélagiennes' and 'L'activité doctrinale dans l'Eglise gallo-romaine,' by

the same author, in A. Fliche and V. Martin, *Histoire de l'Eglise* 4 (Paris 1937) 79 ff., 397 ff. For the canons of the Council of Carthage, cf. Mansi 3. 810-23 (still called there 'Milevitanum') = Hefele-Leclercq 2. 1. 190-6 = ES 101-8.

[3] Cf. St. Augustine, *Epist.* 217 (*Ad Vital.*) and 194 (*Ad Sixt.*).

[4] Cf., e.g. *Epist.* 186 (*Ad Paulin.*) 7. 25 f.

[5] Published in 426 or 427. Cf. also *Epist.* 214 and 215 (*Ad Valent.*).

[6] Published in 426 or 427. Cf. the annotated edition by C. Boyer in *Textus et documenta, ser. theol.* (Rome 1932).

[7] At the time of the *Congregatio de auxiliis* (1598-1607). Cf. M. Jacquin, 'A quelle date parut le terme "sémi-pélagien"?' in *Rev. sc. phil. théol.* 1 (1907) 506-8. For the doctrinal history of Semi-Pelagianism, cf. E. Amann, 'Sémi-Pélagiens,' DTC 14.2 (1941) 1796-850. The expression *reliquiæ pelagianorum* takes its origin from St. Prosper who calls the doctrines of St. Augustine's opponents *pelagianae pravitatis reliquiae: Epist. ad Aug.* 7. It may be good to recall that the term 'Semi-Pelagianism' is historically a misnomer. None of the Semi-Pelagians ever had, or wished to have, any share in Pelagius' doctrines; both Cassian and Faustus of Riez protested that they condemned his errors with the Church. They were in no way half-converted Pelagians. Cf. O. Chadwick. *John Cassian. A Study in Primitive Monasticism* (Cambridge 1950) 113.

[8] Augustinism or St. Augustine's teaching on grace and liberty taken as a whole (cf. E. Portalié, 'Augustinisme, II,' DTC 1. 2 [1903] 2515 ff.), has been understood in different ways according to the different spirit that guides the interpretation of St. Augustine's writings. Some insist more on material faithfulness to the letter; e.g. O. Rotmanner, *Der Augustinismus, eine dogmengeschichtliche Studie* (Munich 1892), as trans. and pref. by J. Liebaert, *Mél. sc. rel.* 6 (1949) 29-48, brings out the points of doctrine in which St. Augustine has not been followed by the Church; thus, in connection with our subject, his teaching on predestination for heaven and hell, and his interpretation of the Scripture text, 1 Tim. 2. 4, on God's salvific will in a restrictive sense. Others endeavour rather to reveal the *spirit* of his system and its fundamental agreement with the Church's doctrine even in the matter of predestination and salvific will, in spite of some unfortunate expressions or an unhappy insistence on one aspect of the question. Cf., e.g. C. Boyer, 'Le système de Saint Augustin sur la grâce,' *Rech. sc. rel.* 20 (1930) 501-25, reprinted in the volume of *Essais sur la doctrine de*

*Saint Augustin* (Paris 1932) 206-36; or H. Rondet, 'L'anthropologie religieuse de Saint Augustin,' *Rech. sc. rel.* 29 (1939) 188-96.

[9] Cf. Amann, *art. cit.* 1819-27 and 1833-49.

[10] The works of St. Prosper are found in ML 51.

[11] ML 51. 67-71 or ML 33. 1002-7 = A. Goldbacher, CSEL 57. 454-68.

[12] ML 33. 1007-12 = CSEL 57. 468-81.

[13] Both written in 428 or 429. For the contents, cf. N. Merlin, *Saint Augustin et les dogmes du péché originel et de la grâce* (Paris 1931) 310-46.

[14] Cf., e.g. *De praed. sanct.* 2. 3. St. Prosper will follow this example of argumentation in the *Contra collatorem* (6 and 14) or the *Carmen de ingratis* (e.g. 126-46; the burden of the whole poem is to show that the Semi-Pelagians logically follow Pelagius); cf. also *De voc.* 1. 22.

[15] *Collationes;* text in ML 49. 477-1326 and in M. Petschenig, CSEL 13. Cassian's Semi-Pelagianism is especially manifest in the 13th Conference (ML 49. 897-954 = CSEL 13. 361-96), which is taken to task by St. Prosper in his *De gratia et libero arbitrio liber contra collatorem* (ML 51. 215-74). On Cassian, cf. L. Cristiani, *Jean Cassien* (2 vols., Paris 1946); Chadwick, *op. cit.*; for his spiritual doctrine, M. Olphé-Galliard, 'Cassien,' DSAM 2 (1938) 214-75.

[16] Text (ML 50. 637-86) by R. S. Moxon, in Cambridge Patristic Texts (Cambridge 1915). On the author and purpose of this treatise, cf. Amann, *art. cit.* 1819-22. St. Vincent's opposition to Augustinism was confined to the doctrine of grace. On that of the Trinity and the Incarnation he was an admirer of St. Augustine as is apparent from a recently discovered work of his: cf. J. Madoz, 'Un tradado desconocido de San Vicente de Lerins,' *Gregorianum* 21 (1940) 75-94; and *Excerpta Vincentii Lirinensis,* in Estudios Onienses, ser. I. 1 (Madrid 1940).

[17] Cf. St. Prosper's *Pro Augustino responsiones ad capitula obiectionum Vincentianarum*: ML 51. 177-86.

[18] Text, ML 51. 205-12 = ES 129-42. Cf. Amann, *art. cit.* 1828-30, on the meaning of the document. St. Prosper's authorship was proved by M. Cappuyns, 'L'origine des capitula pseudo-célestiniens contre le sémi-pélagianisme,' *Rev. Bén.* 41 (1929) 156-70.— L. Cristiani, *op. cit.* (2. 240), characterizes the three respective positions in the question of grace involved in the controversies as follows: To the question, what is man after the Fall able to do

by himself (without grace) in view of his eternal salvation, Pelagius answers that he can do everything; St. Augustine, that he can do nothing; the Semi-Pelagians, that he can do something.

[19] Text in ML 58. 783-836, and A. Engelbrecht, CSEL 21. 1-98. Cf. Amann, *art. cit.* 1833-7.

[20] Cf. 1. 11, '. . . fatalis persuasio quae vim praescientiae cogentis inducit, omnino respuenda est'; also 2. 4. Cf. Amann, *art. cit.* 1836.

[21] St. Fulgentius' reply to Faustus' *De gratia Dei* has not been preserved, but is known from his *Epist. ad Ioan. et Vener.* (ML 45. 435-42) and from a treatise, *De veritate praedestinationis* (*ibid.* 603-72). Cf. Amann, *art. cit.* 1840.

[22] In Mansi 8. 712-8 = Hefele-Leclercq 2. 2. 1085-109. Cf. M. Cappuyns, 'L'origine de capitula d'Orange 529,' *Rech. théol. anc. méd.* 6 (1934) 121-42. According to Cappuyns, canons 1-8 come from John Maxentius (of whom fragments of works are found in MG 86. 1. 75-158). The *capitula* 9-25 are taken from St. Prosper's *Liber sententiarum ex Augustino delibatarum.*

[23] St. Caesarius' sermons in ML 39 and 67 = G. Morin, *Sancti Caesarii Arelatensis Sermones* (2 vols., Maredsous 1937). On Caesarius, cf. P. Lejay, 'Césaire d'Arles (Saint),' DTC 2. 2 (1910) 2168-85, which summarizes the same author's study, 'Le rôle théologique de Césaire d'Arles,' *Rev. d'hist. et de lit. rel.* 10 (1905) 217-66.

[24] ML 51. 427-96. As noted by Cappuyns, 'Le premier représentant de l'augustinisme médiéval, Prosper d'Aquitaine,' *Rech. théol. anc. méd.* 1 (1929) 309-37, this *Liber sententiarum* is the first sample of a type of literature much in fashion in the Middle Ages. (Further references to this article will be shortened, Cappuyns, 'Premier représentant.')—On St. Augustine's contribution to the final victory over Pelagianism, cf. K. Rahner, 'Augustin und der Semipelagianismus,' *Zeitschr. kath. Theol.* (1938) 171-96.

[25] Cf. Amann, *art. cit.* 1830.

[26] Cf. M. Cappuyns, 'L'auteur du De vocatione omnium gentium,' *Rev. Bén.* 39 (1927) 198-226. Further references to this study will be shortened, Cappuyns, 'L'auteur.' The uncertainty about the author of the *De vocatione* originates, no doubt, from the widespread fashion of the time by which writers concealed their authorship either in anonymity or under another well-known author's name. Cf. J. de Ghellinck, *Patristique et Moyen Age* 2 (Brussels-Paris 1947) 351 f.

[27] Cappuyns, 'L'auteur' 199, enumerates six codices with St. Ambrose's name, of which two of the sixteenth century are posterior to the 1492 edition of St. Ambrose's works (Amerbach, Basel). One more was known by ancient cataloguers. He briefly sketches the history of this MS-attribution of the *De vocatione* to St. Ambrose; it appears to originate from one codex *Vat. Lat.* 268, as the Ballerini already believed (cf. ML 55. 159).

[28] Cf. Cappuyns, 'L'auteur' 198 n. 2. Cappuyns mentions (*ibid.* n. 1) other conjectures about the author, pointing to Eucher of Lyons, or Prosper of Orleans. Cf. Quesnel (ML 55. 340-4) or the Ballerini (ML 55. 371-3).

[29] P. Quesnel, *Dissertatio secunda de auctore librorum de vocatione omnium gentium*, in vol. 2 of *S. Leonis opera omnia*, Paris, 1675; Lyons, 1700. This dissertation was reprinted in ML 55. 339-72. Quesnel admitted that the accepted opinion considered St. Prosper as the author; the heading of his *dissertatio* continues, *qui Prospero Aquitano vulgo attribuuntur.* He also attests, *op. cit.* 18 (ML 55. 361), that before him reasons for doubting St. Prosper's authorship had been proposed by G. J. Vossius, *Historiae de controversiis quas Pelagius eiusque reliquiae moverunt: Lib. VII* (Amsterdam 1655) 1. 20; and by H. de Noris, *Historia Pelagiana* (Padua 1673) 2. 14. Cf. Cappuyns, 'L'auteur' 201 n. 3. Quesnel's edition of St. Leo was put on the Index on account of the Jansenistic ideas expressed in his annotations (cf. a description of his edition in the *Schoenemanni notitia historico-litteraria in S. Leonem*, in ML 54. 82-6). A new edition of St. Leo was then prepared by the brothers J. and P. Ballerini (cf. below, n. 32) by commission of, and with the financial support of, Pope Benedict XIV to whom they dedicate their work.

It should be noted that Quesnel's argument from internal evidence for the Leonine composition of the *De vocatione* is weak when we consider the fact of Prosper's influence in St. Leo's writings, which is generally admitted. Cf. de Ghellinck, *op. cit.* 213 f., and below, n. 44.

[30] J. Antelmi, *De veris operibus SS. Patrum Leonis Magni et Prosperi Aquitani dissertationes criticae*, Paris, 1869; cf. the Ballerini in ML 55. 373 f., and Cappuyns, 'L'auteur' 198 n. 1. Antelmi's hypothesis that the treatise had been published anonymously, was also proposed by Quesnel, *op. cit.* 12 (ML 55. 345 f.).

[31] L. E. Du Pin, *Nouvelle bibliothèque des auteurs ecclésiastiques* (Paris 1695) 4. 199 ff. The *Admonitio in libros de vocatione om-*

*nium gentium,* printed in ML 51. 639-48, is the Latin translation of Du Pin's article. Cf. Cappuyns, 'L'auteur' 199 n. 1.

[32] *Ballerinorum observationes in dissertationem secundam Quesnelli de auctore librorum de vocatione omnium gentium,* in vol. 2 of *S. Leonis opera,* Venice, 1756 = ML 55. 371-88. They conjectured as author an unknown Prosper, other than St. Prosper of Aquitaine; cf. ML 55. 160. The *Schoenemanni notitia hist.-litt.* gives a glowing description of their edition of St. Leo's works, ML 54. 97-103.

[33] Cf. O. Bardenhewer, *Geschichte der altkirchlichen Literatur* 4 (Freiburg i. B. 1924) 541 f.; J. Tixeront, *A Handbook of Patrology* (4th ed. trans. by S. A. Raemers, St. Louis 1927) 272; A Cayré, *Patrologie et histoire de la théologie* (4th ed. Tournai 1947) 2. 186. Yet, cf. Amann, *art. cit.* 1832: 'The question of the author seems to tend towards a definite solution.' The solution he expects to become definite is the one of Cappuyns.

[34] 'L'auteur,' etc.—cf. above, n. 26.

[35] Cappuyns, 'L'auteur' 200, enumerates ten extant MSS which attribute the *De vocatione* to St. Prosper, and mentions six more that were known by ancient editors or authors. He concludes: 'L'attribution à Prosper n'est pas un fait isolé au XII^e siècle et se rencontre déja en Allemagne au IX-X^e siècle.'

[36] ML 121. 276: 'De hac iterum dispensatione divinorum operum Prosper in libro de vocatione gentium ita loquitur . . . .' This is followed by the quotation, 'Multa enim sunt . . .,' comprising the entire ch. 14 of Book One.

[37] ML 125. 203 D-4 A: 'Prosper in libro secunda de vocatione gentium demonstrat dicens . . .,' with quotation from ch. 8.: 'Non omnis reparabilis reparatus . . . .' till 'gratia est.'

[38] Cappuyns, 'L'auteur' 201 n. 1.

[39] Cappuyns, *ibid.* 201.

[40] Cappuyns concludes a close examination (*ibid.* 202-12) of the doctrinal parallelism between St. Prosper and the *De vocatione* thus (212), 'We have found no real difference in doctrine.' As examples of this identity of doctrine he gives the following: both affirm a universal salvific will, both refer this fact to God's general mercies, both sacrifice partly the Augustinian predestination and lay greater stress on human freedom. In both we find the same incoherences and the same original line of evolution.

[41] The literary comparison is found in pp. 213-20 of Cappuyns' 'L'auteur.'

[42] Cf. Cappuyns, *ibid.* 214 f. and n. 1 of 214.

[43] *Ibid.* 220.—Independently of Cappuyns' study and as communicated in writing to the present translator, P. Schepens (+1950), in an unpublished comparative study of the vocabulary of St. Prosper and the *De vocatione,* had arrived at the same conclusion about the author of our treatise.

[44] Cappuyns, 'L'auteur' 220-5. Compare the title page of ML 51: *S. Prosperi Aquitani S. Augustini discipuli S. Leonis papae notarii* . . . . For the parallel passages pointed out by Quesnel, cf. his *dissertatio* (ML 55. 351-4).

[45] E.g. G. Bardy, 'Prosper d'Aquitaine (Saint),' DTC 13.1 (1936) 847. In his revised edition of P. de Labriolle's *Histoire de la littérature latine chrétienne* (Paris 1947) 2. 666 n., Bardy writes: 'Il est *actuellement démontré* que saint Prosper est encore l'auteur du *De Vocatione omnium gentium.*' See also B. Steidle, *Patrologie* (Freiburg i. B. 1937) 96; B. Altaner, *Patrologie* (2nd ed. Freiburg i. B. 1950) 400: the work can be attributed to Prosper 'with great probability.' L. Pelland, *S. Prosperi Aquitani doctrina de praedestinatione et voluntate salvifica, de eius in augustinismum influxu* (Montreal 1936) 154, believes, 'solida cum probabilitate posse hos libros *De voc. omn. gent.* Prospero Aquitano attribui.' Cf. J. Gaidioz, 'Saint Prosper d'Aquitaine et le tome à Flavien,' *Rev. sc. rel.* 23 (1949) 270-301, esp. 287 ff.—In order to confirm the conclusion that St. Prosper is the author of the *De vocatione,* we shall frequently refer in the notes to parallel or identical texts in his other works.

[46] Cf. G. Bardy, *art. cit.,* who utilizes the preceding studies on Prosper, especially the two articles of Cappuyns frequently quoted here. Cf. also L. Valentin, *Saint Prosper d'Aquitaine, étude sur la littérature latine ecclésiastique au V^e siècle en Gaule* (Paris 1900), and his reviewer, L. Couture, in two articles: 'Saint Prosper d'Aquitaine,' *Bull. litt. ecclés.* (1900) 269-82 and (1901) 33-49; M. Jacquin, 'La question de la prédestination au V^e et VI^e siècles,' *Rev. hist. ecclés.* (1906) 269-300.

[47] Except for slight discrepancies which do not affect Prosper's doctrinal evolution, scholars agree on the chronology of his works. Cf. below, n. 52.

[48] Thus Valentin, Couture, Jacquin, Bardy, Amann, Cayré, Cappuyns.

[49] Jacquin, *art. cit.,* holds that St. Prosper abandoned St. Augustine's teaching in one point only, and brought in an innovation

by explaining reprobation *post praevisa merita*. This can be seen, for instance, in *Resp. cap. Gall.* 3: 'Ideo praesdestinati non sunt, quia tales futuri ex voluntaria praevaricatione praesciti sunt.' Cappuyns, 'Premier représentant,' admits a more general evolution in St. Prosper's doctrinal positions, in a direction away from Augustinism; so, too, Amann, *art. cit.* 1827: 'V. Le repli des augustiniens'; and several others. Pelland, *op. cit.*, refuses to believe that St. Prosper ever ceased to be a faithful follower of St. Augustine. These differences in interpretation arise partly from the different conceptions of Augustine's doctrine and of Augustinism. Cf. above, n. 8.

[50] We shall frequently indicate in the notes parallel passages in St. Augustine's works, drawing mainly from those written at the time of the Pelagian and Semi-Pelagian controversies (412-30), and only occasionally from his other writings. It will thus be seen that these are incomparably more numerous than the few similar texts which Quesnel detected between St. Leo and the *De vocatione*. This will be at the same time an additional proof to exclude Quesnel's supposition that Leo must be the the the author of our treatise. For St. Leo, as is well known, was never influenced by St. Augustine, in his ideas and their expression, to the extent that one can perceive the Augustinian influence at work in the *De vocatione*; whilst St. Prosper in all his works does clearly reveal his Augustinism.

[51] 'Premier représentant' 310.

[52] The chronological order of St. Prosper's works, according to Cappuyns, *art. cit.*, is as follows. First period (till about 432): 1) *Epistola ad Rufinum de gratia et libero arbitrio* (426-427); 2) *Epistola ad Augustinum* (end of 428); 3) *Carmen de ingratis* (about 430), a versified rendering of the *Epist. ad Ruf.*, with a pun on the *ingrati*—'ungrateful' and 'enemies of grace' (inspired by St. Augustine, *Serm.* 26. 11. 14, 'contra istam gratiam ab ingratis non disputetur'); 4) *Pro Augustino responsiones ad excerpta Genuensium* (after 430). Of this last work G. de Plinval, *Pélage* 367 n. 1, ventures a possible correction of the title, *Agenuensium* = 'the men of Agen,' instead of *Genuensium*. Valentin, Couture, Jacquin, Pelland, Amann invert the order of *Epist. ad Ruf.* and *Epist. ad Aug.*— Second period (433-435): 1) *De gratia et libero arbitrio liber contra collatorem*, a heated and not always fair attack on Cassian (see Chadwick, *op. cit.* 135); 2) *Pro Augustino responsiones ad capitula obiectionum Gallorum calumniantium*; 3) *Pro Augustino responsiones ad capitula obiectionum Vincentianarum*. Valentin and Cou-

ture invert this order and place the *Contra coll.* after both series of *Responsiones.* Jacquin here agrees with Cappuyns, but places the *Resp. excerp. Gen.* in this period.—Third period (after 435, date of Cassian's death, when Prosper resides in Rome): 1) *Expositio in Psalmos* (between 435 and 449), a summary of St. Augustine's *Enarr. in Ps.;* 2) *Capitula, seu praeteritorum Sedis Apostolicae episcoporum auctoritates de gratia Dei* (between 435 and 442); 3) LIBRI DUO DE VOCATIONE OMNIUM GENTIUM (about 450); 4) *Liber sententiarum ex Augustino delibatarum* (about 451); 5) *Epigrammata ex sententiis S. Augustini* (after 451), the previous work in verse; 6) St. Prosper's *Chronicum,* begun before 435 during his stay in Gaul and continued in Rome, stops at the year 455. Cappuyns concludes that he must have died shortly after this date.

Even for scholars who hesitate to subscribe to Cappuyns' conclusion about St. Prosper's authorship of the *De vocatione,* our treatise finds its historical setting in the evolution of Augustinism at the moment when the Catholic doctrine began to be separated from Augustinian theories. Whether written by Prosper or not, the *De vocatione* is the fruit and a symptom of a partial withdrawal of the Augustinians. Cf. Amann, *art. cit.* 1827. This is exactly St. Prosper's position in his last period, as Cappuyns, 'Premier représentant,' has clearly shown.

[53] Several authors writing on the *De vocatione* summarize Book One by saying that it deals with the gratuitousness of grace; cf. Amann, *art cit.* 1831, or L. Capéran, *Le problème du salut des infidèles. Essai historique* (2d ed. Paris 1934) 138. This may be correct as to the material contents of the Book, but it hardly corresponds to the author's purpose and to the formal viewpoint he takes. He intends to study the universal salvific will, *De vocatione OMNIUM GENTIUM.* Only in order to expose this doctrine 'which cannot be denied' (1. 1) and to reconcile it with the fact that many are not saved, he brings in the doctrine about the gratuitousness of grace. Cf. in this sense Pelland, *op. cit.* 157.

[54] For St. Augustine's interpretation of 1 Tim. 2. 4 (or of similar texts) cf. E. Portalié, 'Augustin (Saint),' DTC 1. 2 (1903) 2407, or Capéran, *op. cit.* 197-9. St. Augustine, as is well known, interpreted the text in a restrictive meaning in at least three different ways: cf. *Enchir.* 27. 103 (ACW 4. 97 and n. 336); *De corrept. et grat.* 15. 47; *De praed. sanct.* 8. 14.—For a brief historical survey of medieval Augustinism, cf. A. d'Alès, 'Prédestination,' DAFC 4

(1922) 216-25. After Cappuyns' studies on the *De vocatione,* the reference to its 'anonymous author' needs revision.

⁵⁵ Cf. Cassian, *Coll.* 13, *De prov. div.* 7. Cf. St. Prosper's *Epist. ad Aug.* 4, and Hilary's *Epist. ad Aug.* 7.

⁵⁶ Even to-day scholars do not agree in their way of interpreting the *De vocatione.* Does it hold universalism or particularism of God's salvific will? Some, as for instance, A. d'Alès, *art. cit.* 216, read in it an indubitable universalism. So did Portalié, 'Augustinisme,' DTC 1. 2 (1903) 2525 f. Others, e.g. Jacquin, *art. cit.* 293, refuse to read in St. Prosper's works a genuinely unrestricted universal will of salvation. A key to this diversity of opinions may perhaps be discovered in Amann, *art. cit.* 1832, when he says that the doctrine of the *De vocatione* is to some extent inconsistent in its diverse affirmations, owing to the 'fluctuations of a thought of which cohesion is not the most outstanding feature.' The author of the *De vocatione* sees in each of the opposing systems of St. Augustine and the Semi-Pelagians what are their good and weak points; from both sides he takes what he thinks right, and rejects what he considers unacceptable, without realizing that by so doing he constructs a system that harbours inconsistencies and contradictions. (Cappuyns, 'L'auteur' 212, also notes these incoherences.) This view may be the closest to the objective facts given by the texts. It also allows a more natural interpretation of various statements which it is then not necessary to force into a firmly coherent structure. But the desire of the author to open out a more pronounced universalism than he had read in St. Augustine seems to be beyond doubt. It will have to be seen in detail how far he is successful in executing this desire.

⁵⁷ A clear expression of this connection between the gratuitousness of grace and predestination is found, for example, in *De dono persev.* 13. 33.

⁵⁸ This brief summary of Book One may fail to bring out sufficiently the formal viewpoint of St. Prosper in dealing at length with the gratuitousness of grace. The text itself interspersed with repeated mention of the universal salvific will (1. 5, 12, 20, 25) manifests his intention more clearly. His study of the gratuitousness of grace, aimed undoubtedly at the Semi-Pelagians, is loosened from its connection with predestination, and answers the question why it is that not all are saved. The Semi-Pelagians answered the question by saying that those perish who do not wish to be saved,

stressing the fact that grace waits for their initiative. St. Prosper wanted to discard this explanation at any cost.

[59] The universal distribution of grace is in no way opposed to its gratuitous character. Cf., e.g. a modern theologian, H. Rondet, 'La grâce libératrice,' *Nouv. rev. théol.* 69 (1947) 128 f. St. Prosper, as has just been said, has his own reason for insisting on the complete gratuitousness of grace: he writes against the Semi-Pelagians.

[60] Those authors especially who maintain that St. Prosper never swerved from St. Augustine's teaching, find in the Doctor of Grace an equivalent to St. Prosper's distinction between general and special grace. Already Portalié, *art. cit.*, DTC 1. 2. 2407 f., leads up to it when he sees in St. Augustine's interpretation given in the *De spir. et. litt.* 33. 58, a universal but conditional salvific will (corresponding to St. Prosper's *gratia generalis*, and, for Portalié, the equivalent of the *voluntas antecedens* of later Scholasticism) and in the later interpretations of 1 Tim. 2. 4 the efficacious salvific will which applies only to the elect (the equivalent of the *gratia specialis* of the *De vocatione,* and of the *voluntas consequens* of the Scholastics). There may be a real, but implicit and incomplete, correspondence. On the idea of universal grace in St. Augustine, cf. de Plinval, *Pélage* 399 f.

[61] Cf. Cappuyns, 'L'auteur' 222. Quesnel found in St. Leo the idea of a general help offered and given to all men in the following seven passages: *Serm.* 18. 2, 19. 2, 35. 4, 38. 3, 44. 1, 82. 2, 91. 1. Cappuyns, *ibid.* 224, notes more parallel expressions (e.g. *Serm.* 24. 1, 67. 1), and points out the different doctrinal context. St. Leo gives expression to the idea, but does not connect it with the salvific will; he does not go beyond St. Paul's idea in Rom. 1. 20 f.

[62] For a detailed discussion of the *gratia generalis* and *specialis,* cf. below, Book Two n. 226, where references to the text are given for every particular statement.

[63] Cf. below, Book Two nn. 210-16.

[64] On the doctrine of election or predestination in the *De vocatione,* cf. n. 316 to Book Two.

[65] This important element for the solution of our problem is insinuated rather than explicitly stated, but it is scarcely made use of— owing, no doubt, to the fact that our author is obsessed by the election theory: cf. below, Book Two n. 232.

[66] Thus Cappuyns, 'Premier représentant' 337, 'Aussi bien l'universalisme de Prosper . . . se réduit-il au dernière analyse à une excellente intention.' Perhaps this conclusion should be slightly

modified, and in the light of n. 56, a more real universalism may be said to have been affirmed by St. Prosper; provided, however, we do not require too stringent a consistency of the system found in the *De vocatione*. He really intends to establish a universal salvific will which excludes no man and extends grace to all men, no one being excepted. And he means to say explicitly that all men do receive grace. Yet it is clear that grace which actually leads to salvation is not received by all, for not all are saved. Why does their grace not save them? Here lies the mystery; for St. Prosper the answer is hidden in God's judgments—His election.

⁶⁷ No one denies that St. Prosper softens down St. Augustine's excessively rigid *expressions;* the purposeful avoidance of the words 'predestination' and its derived forms (it occurs only once, in a Scripture quotation) is too clear a proof of this. As noted above, n. 56, not all students of Prosper agree that he would also have interpreted some of St. Augustine's *ideas* on predestination and salvific will in a more lenient sense. We are inclined to think that there is a real change in the viewpoint and in the stress laid on different aspects of the mystery of man's salvation, and, consequently, a change, at least to some extent, in the ideas themselves. If we do not demand absolute consistency of system in the *De vocatione*, as in the whole of St. Prosper's theology, we may frankly admit a veering away from St. Augustine's ideas in the conception of the universal salvific will. Yet at the same time he tries to hold on to a theory of election that does not go together with his universalism. At any rate, the *De vocatione* remains 'another attempt to temper the Augustinian teaching' (Cayré, *Manual of Patrology* 2 [tr. by H. Howitt, Tournai 1940] 190).

⁶⁸ Thus Cappuyns, Valentin, d'Alès, Amann, Capéran, Tixeront, etc.

⁶⁹ St. Prosper's influence, though real in the early Middle Ages (cf. Cappuyns, 'Premier représentant' 335 n. 82) is less felt in the golden age of Scholasticism. St. Thomas, for example, seems to have known only or mainly his *Liber sent. ex Aug. delib.* This may be partly due to the fact, recently pointed out by H. Bouillard, *Conversion et grâce chez S. Thomas d'Aquin, Etude historique* (Paris 1944), that the historical Semi-Pelagianism and the canons of the Council of Orange that condemned it were practically unknown by the Scholastics from the twelfth to the sixteenth century. These canons were not in the council collections in use at the time, up to 1538, when they were inserted in a new edition of the councils by Peter Crabbe, Cologne. Till then the theologians were unac-

quainted with the Council of Orange itself. Cf. Bouillard, *op. cit.*
92-122: 'Découverte du semi-pélagianisme.'—To-day the *De vocatione* finds honourable mention in most theological or historical
surveys of the problem of the salvation of infidels. Cf., e.g. Capéran, *op. cit.* 137-43, or d'Alès, *art. cit.* 1156-81. A recent study by
I. Ortega, *De vocatione omnium gentium in salutem* (Manila 1946)
87, mentions our treatise in its historical survey, with too laudatory
an appreciation of it: 'catholicam doctrinam ita insigniter confecit
ut addendum vix quidquam appareat.'

[70] With the title, *De vocatione omnium gentium libri duo qui
Leoni Magno a Quesnello perperam attributi ignoto cuidam Prospero adiudicandi videntur* (cf. above, n. 29 and n. 32). The Ballerini text of the *De vocatione,* which was not reprinted in Migne
with their text of St. Leo, improves Mangeant's edition (for which
cf. the foll. n.) by a further collation of three MSS: *Vat. Reg.* 293,
*Vat. Lat.* 268, and *Vat. Lat.* 262 (cf. ML 55. 157-9). The Ballerini,
*loc cit.,* cite three more MSS of the *De vocatione* that bear St. Prosper's name, *Vat. Palat.* 236, *Vat. Lat.* 558, and *Vat. Lat.* 559, and
a fourth under St. Ambrose's name, *Vat. Lat.* 281, which, however,
they did not use to establish their text.

[71] Mangeant's text, prepared by le Brun des Marettes and D.
Mangeant, is based on the printed editions of St. Prosper's works
of Louvain (1565, by J. Soteaux), Douai (1577, by J. Olivier), and
Cologne (1609, reproduces Douai), which they corrected with the
assistance of Quesnel's edition of the *De vocatione* in the *Opera
S. Leonis* (this itself was mainly made on a MS *Par. Nat.* 2156 =
the *Codex Thuaneus* of ML 51) and through collation of two more
MSS, one of the *Codex Camberonensis,* known but not used for
the revision of the text by J. Olivier for the Douai edition, and the
*Par. Nat.* 17413 (= *Codex Joliensis*). Cf. ML 51. 649 A and
55. 157 f.; and Cappuyns, 'L'auteur' 200 n. 1.—H. Hurter has the *De
vocatione* in vol. 3 of the *SS. PP. opuscula selecta,* with only a few
variant readings from the Ballerini text. ML 17 prints a text of the
*De vocatione* among the doubtful or spurious works of St. Ambrose
(1073-132); it was added by Migne to the Benedictine edition of
St. Ambrose's works which he was reprinting, without any indication of its source. This text has a different division into chapters,
only nine for Book One and ten for Book Two.

[72] In the notes B stands for the Ballerini text and M for Mangeant's (Migne 51).

[73] The translation is mentioned in the *Schoenemanni notitia his-*

*torico-litteraria in S. Prosperum,* printed in Migne's volume of St. Prosper's works (ML 51. 61). The rare work is found in the Bibliothèque Nationale of Paris from where a copy of it on microfilm was obtained. For the author of that translation, Antoine Girard, cf. C. Sommervogel, *Bibliothèque des écrivains de la Compagnie de Jésus* 3. 1434-43. The *Vocation des Gentils* is mentioned 1439. 14 *bis.* It was published without the name of the translator, as more books and translations of A. Girard had been. Girard's remarks are mainly levelled against the Jansenists.—The French translation of St. Prosper's works published by P. Lequeux, Paris, 1762, does not give the *De vocatione.* This translator included only the works that definitely belong (or were considered as belonging) to St. Prosper, and after Quesnel's *dissertatio* the once accepted opinion was no longer commonly held. A. Girard who came before Quesnel, considered St. Prosper as the author of the *De vocatione.*

## BOOK ONE

[1] *defensores liberi arbitrii* = the *Massilienses,* later known as the Semi-Pelagians; *praedicatores gratiae Dei* = the followers of St. Augustine. The text refers to the first phase of the Semi-Pelagian and Augustinian controversies, the acme of which was reached in the years 430-5, with Cassian and St. Vincent of Lerins on the Semi-Pelagian side, and St. Prosper of Aquitaine as their chief opponent. Cf. Intro. 4-6.

[2] The *De vocatione* affirms universalism in God's salvific will, which is taken as certain or even as of faith (cf. below, ch. 25): it departs in this view from St. Augustine's restrictive interpretations of 1 Tim. 2. 4 (cf., however, below—chs. 9-12). Cf. Prosper in *Resp. cap. Vincent.* 2: 'Sincerissime credendum atque profitendum est Deum velle ut omnes homines salvi fiant'; and *Resp. cap. Gall.* 8. Jacquin, 'La question de la prédestination au V^e et VI^e siècles,' *Rev. hist. eccl.* 7 (1906) 293, does admit here a real universalism. Cf. Cappuyns, 'L'auteur' 206 f.

[3] Cf. St. Augustine, *Enarr. in Ps.* 70. 2. 1: 'Gratia gratis data est. Nam nisi gratis esset, gratia non esset'; and *Retract.* 1. 22. 2: 'Non est gratia, si eam ulla merita praecedunt . . . .' The dilemma is clearly stated. If God wills the salvation of all men, why are not

all actually saved? Either because of the will of men, but then
grace without which there is no salvation is made dependent on the
merits of men and it is no longer a gift but something due to men;
or because of the will of God who does not give grace to some men,
but then there seems to be no universal salvific will, since God
would not give to all the only means of salvation—which He alone
can give—grace. The latent presupposition of the dilemma is the
Augustinian idea that God's will and grace are always effective of
their purpose. Later theology will distinguish two kinds of divine
will and of grace, and thus evade the dilemma. St. Augustine, as is
well known (cf. Amann, *art. cit.* 1814), avoided to treat *ex professo*
of the salvific will, and in his later years at least interpreted the
relevant Scripture texts in a particularistic sense.

⁴ An often recurring principle of solution for the problem studied
in the *De vocatione* is stated here: it is necessary to clearly distinguish between what we are able to know and what is beyond
our ken (cf. Book Two, ch. 1). This reference to the unknowable
mystery of God's judgments is Augustinian: cf., e.g. *De corrept. et
grat.* 8. 17; and Amann, *art. cit.* 1802. St. Prosper insists more particularly on the necessity of discerning between the mystery and
what we can come to know. Cf. below, Book Two n. 290.

⁵ *annitar inquirere*: in this phrase Quesnel, *Dissertatio 2a* (ML
55. 345 f.), and the Ballerini, *Observationes in diss. 2a* (*ibid.* 373),
read an indication that it is the first time the author of the *De
vocatione* treats of this problem; that he, therefore, cannot be St.
Prosper of Aquitaine. This conclusion seems to be unwarranted,
when we consider his purpose, expressly stated here: to determine
what can and what cannot be known in the matter. Would it not
be more correct to say that this is possible only, or, at any rate,
will be better done, if done by one who has dealt with these
problems before and is familiar with them?

⁶ This limit of our knowledge will repeatedly be pointed out; cf.
below, chs. 13, 14, 21, 25.

⁷ ... *de* ... *motibus et gradibus voluntatis:* lit., the 'movements'
of the will at its different levels or degrees. Cf. below, ch. 2, the
threefold will in man.

⁸ Pelagius' conception of freedom (cf., e.g. St. Augustine, *Opus
imp. c. Iul.* 6. 9, Julian's explanation: '... possibilitas peccandi et
non peccandi ... quae habeat facultatem in quod voluerit latus
suopte insistendi arbitratu') according to which he is free who
can do what he wants, requires that man is equally able to do good

or evil. Consequently, if a man is not able to do good by himself, without grace, this would mean that he is not free. The Semi-Pelagians did not go that far (cf., however, Cassian, in St. Prosper's *Contra coll.* 13. 6), but they objected to the initiative being taken by grace; if the will is set in motion by grace, it does not move itself, and would then not be free. Cf. the following note.

[9] *non ducem sed comitem:* grace not preceding or leading, but following, the will. This expresses exactly the Semi-Pelagian position; cf. Cassian, *Coll.* 13. 11. Cassian taught, it should be noted, that the initiative for good works at times belongs to our human will and at other times to grace; cf. Amann, *art. cit.* 1806-8. Note also Prosper, *Epist. ad Aug.* 5: '. . . gratiam Dei, quam comitem, non praeviam humanorum volunt esse meritorum.' Compare St. Augustine, *Epist.* 186 (*Ad Paulin.*) 3. 10: '. . . comitante, non ducente, pedisequa, non praevia voluntate.' St. Augustine's answer to the Semi-Pelagian position was already noted (above, n. 3); cf. also *Epist.* 194 (*Ad Sixt.*) 3. 14; *De corr. et grat.* 7. 13.

[10] For this argument of the Semi-Pelagians in favour of free will, cf. *Contra coll.* 19: 'Quoniam secundum ipsos, si aufertur liberum arbitrium cum gratia praevenitur, aufertur gratia cum libero arbitrio praevenitur.' No direct answer is given to it here. The *De vocatione* holds the Augustinian view that there can be no true virtues without grace (cf. below, ch. 4). An argument *ad hominem* is, however, sketched here: if grace is not the cause of all merits, it is no longer grace; it would then be due to man for some previous merit. Cf. Rom. 11. 6; St. Augustine, *Epist.* 194 (*Ad Sixt.*) 3. 7.

[11] *naturaliter inest qualiscumque voluntas*: as the three following chapters will show, in St. Prosper's conception the same appetitive faculty in man, called will, is active at three different levels or attains three different degrees of perfection.

[12] For *donum Dei, donum Spiritus (Sancti)*, see J. P. Christopher, ACW 2. 132 n. 222; L. A. Arand, ACW 3. 128 n. 120.

[13] These three degrees of the will are found in St. Prosper's other works, though not brought together as here. Cf. below, nn. 14, 15, 36. St. Augustine has the same conception, but considers especially the last two degrees. Cf. *De civ. Dei* 13. 2, 'Quid sit secundum carnem, quid secundum spiritum vivere'; and 4, 'Quid sit secundum hominem, quid secundum Deum vivere.'

[14] *Voluntas sensualis:* the animal will or the appetitive power that tends spontaneously to sensible objects, as in the irrational animals. It is not *sensual* in the meaning of the English word that connotes

something inordinate or sinful. Scholastic philosophy will call it the sensitive appetitive power and conceive it as distinct from the rational will. Cf. *Contra coll.* 13. 6; the *infantes, excordes et fatui,* are said to have a will but not a *liberum arbitrium.*

[15] *voluntas animalis:* the purely human or natural will, called *animalis,* an echo of St. Paul, 1 Cor. 2. 14, in opposition to the spiritual will (below, ch. 6), not because it aims only at sensible objects, as the animal or sensitive appetite does, which has been called *sensualis* in the previous chapter; but because in all its objects it does not look for a higher spiritual good and remains confined to earthly and perishable things. Cf. Spencer's translation of 1 Cor. 2. 14. It is *natural* in the sense of not supernaturalized or spiritualized. Cf. Girard's French translation, 'volonté naturelle.'

[16] That only a terrestrial reward awaits the good efforts of the natural will, is an Augustinian idea, found especially in St. Augustine's teachings about the virtues of pagans; see, e.g. *De civ. Dei,* 5. 15; also Prosper, *Carm. de ingr.* 401 f., and the text cited in the following note.

[17] Another conception of St. Augustine: reference to God of all good works is necessary to make them truly good and worthy of a lasting reward. Cf. *De spir. et litt.* 27. 48; *Contra Iul. Pelag.* 4. 3. 22. Note, too, Prosper, *Contra coll.* 13. 3: '. . . multi eorum (impiorum) sint iustitiae, temperantiae, continentiae et benevolentiae sectatores; quae omnia non frustra quidem neque inutiliter habent, multumque ex eis in hac vita honoris et gloriae consequuntur; sed quia in his studiis non Deo sed diabolo serviunt, licet habeant temporalem de vana laude mercedem, ad illam tamen beatarum virtutum non pertinent veritatem.'

[18] Rom. 1. 20.—For the Scripture texts of which our author will quote abundantly, we should note at the outset that, as is to be expected of a fifth-century author, St. Prosper cites different versions of the Latin Scriptures, both the Vulgate and the ancient versions, without any rigid consistency. It is not always possible (cf. Cappuyns, 'L'auteur' 214 n. 1), on account of the imperfect state of the edited texts, to determine with accuracy which versions are cited. Broadly speaking, we may say that the New Testament books are generally quoted according to the Vulgate, with occasional inversions in the order of the words and slight variants that hardly affect the meaning. A few exceptions to this rule were pointed out by Cappuyns, *loc. cit.,* as an additional proof of St. Prosper's authorship of the *De vocatione,* the same exceptions occurring in

Prosper's other works. The variant readings are more rarely found for the Gospels and the Acts than for the Epistles of St. Paul and St. John; they are more frequent and more considerable for the two Epistles of St. Peter, so much so that for these especially (and at times also for St. Paul) it is often impossible to say whether the texts are taken from old versions or merely cited in a free way from the Vulgate. Of the Old Testament, the Psalms and Job are consistently quoted according to the Vulgate. Most of the other books are cited from older versions, especially the Prophets, (Jer., Isa., Joel); Prov., Isa., Tob., and Esth. are also (or generally) quoted according to the Septuagint.

[19] Rom. 1. 22.—Cf. *Resp. excerp. Gen.* 8; St. Augustine, *De spir. et litt.* 11. 20.

[20] *Ibid.* 1. 21.

[21] When men rise to the knowledge of the supreme Good, they do not effect this without the help of God's grace—*illuminante Dei gratia*. This might be interpreted to mean that human reason *cannot* come to the knowledge of God without the help of grace. To-day we believe the contrary—cf. ES 1785, 1806. The *De vocatione* only says that in fact grace was given men to come to the knowledge of God. Cf. the theme of Augustine in *De civ. Dei* 11. 2: 'De cognoscendo Deo, ad cuius notitiam nemo hominum pervenit nisi per mediatorem Dei et hominum, hominem Christum Iesum.'

[22] Another Augustinian idea: man cannot be good unless he be led and helped by grace: cf. *De spir. et litt.* 3. 5: 'Neque liberum arbitrium quidquam nisi ad peccandum valet, si lateat veritatis via.' Yet, when a man comes to sin, he is not without guilt, as the following chapter will explain.

[23] Deut. 32. 8 (Septuagint).

[24] Lev. 20. 26.

[25] Esther 10. 9 f. (Sept.).

[26] Acts 14. 14 f.

[27] God elected his chosen people Israel among the nations and guided them by His special Providence, a gift not bestowed on the other peoples. This statement of Scripture does not exclude the general Providence which at all times God has shown for all nations. We have here a first expression of St. Prosper's original contribution to the explanation of the universal salvific will, the distinction between a special and a general Providence and grace (cf. Intro. 15-18). A similar distinction is found in St. Augustine,

especially in his writings previous to the controversies on grace, but without explicit reference to the salvific will. Cf. *De div. quaest.* 83. 44: 'Aliud enim est quod divina providentia quasi privatim cum singulis agit, aliud quod generi universo tamquam publice consulit'; see also *De vera rel.* 25. 46.—The apparent digression of this ch. 5 fits in with our author's treatment of the natural will in man; it explains how the aberrations of the natural will are without excuse.

[28] *elementorum*: 'the things created' (Tertullian, *De ieiun.* 10: sun and moon; *Adv. Hermog.* 31: earth and sky; cf. TLL 5. 2. 346. 51 ff.) which, according to Rom. 1. 20, naturally lead men to the knowledge and worship of their Creator. For a study of the term *elementum*, see H. Diels, *Elementum* (Leipzig 1899).

[29] Is the care of Providence for all men and the gifts His goodness extends to all a *natural* or a *supernatural* help? As is well known, the distinction between natural and supernatural is not as yet explicit at the time of St. Prosper. According to Cappuyns, 'L'auteur' 209, the *generalis gratia* of the *De vocatione* and of St. Prosper's other works is more than a merely natural help. For Pelland, *op. cit.* 166 f., this general Providence does not exclude, it is true, interior graces but leaves these out of consideration; it aims only at the external vocation to the faith. Cf. below, Book Two n. 226.

[30] Cf. St. Paul, Rom. 1. 20-25.

[31] Compare St. Paul, Rom. 3. 9-20. The idea is to bring out that even among the chosen people the just or elect remained so through grace only. Cf. below, n. 34, and above, n. 22. There is no true virtue without grace.

[32] . . . *cui committi non est aliud quam dimitti* = to entrust oneself to the direction of this degenerate will means nothing else than to be forsaken and to go astray. Compare Girard (8), 'pour elle c'est la même chose de faire des chutes, que d'être mise en son pouvoir'; also the Ballerinis' marginal note, 'sibi committi, dimitti est.'

[33] Cf. *Carm. de ingr.* 530.

[34] About this well-known teaching of St. Augustine's that the virtues of pagans are vices, cf. J. Wang-Tch' ang-Tche, *Saint Augustin et les vertus des païens* (Paris 1938). It is evidently to be rightly understood. Taken out of its context this very proposition has been condemned by the Church among the errors of Baius (ES 1025), of the Jansenists (*ibid.* 1298) and of Quesnel (*ibid.* 1388). For St. Augustine, cf., e.g. *De civ. Dei* 19. 25; *Contra Iul. Pelag.* 4. 3. 17; *In Ioan. Ev. tract.* 45. 2; and the penetrating analysis

by J. Mausbach, *Die Ethik des heiligen Augustinus* (2nd ed. Freiburg i. Br. 1929) 2. 258-341: 'Das sittliche Handeln ausserhalb des Christentums und der Kirche.' Prosper proposes the same idea, e.g. in *Contra coll.* 13.3: 'Et ita manifestissime patet, in impiorum animis nullam habitare virtutem, sed omnia opera eorum immunda esse atque polluta.' Cf. *Carm. de ingr.* 406-9.

[35] This is the catholic teaching, that the beginning of all good, the will for good, comes from grace and not from man's initiative (the famous *initium fidei*). The Semi-Pelagian position of Cassian held that God waits and sees till we wish to turn to good works, and then comes and strengthens us with His grace, as the Lord did with Zachaeus: cf. *Coll.* 13. 11. Regarding this *bona voluntas*, see St. Augustine, *De grat. et lib. arb.* 15. 31. On the Semi-Pelagian meaning of *initium fidei*, cf. J. Chéné, 'Que signifiait "initium fidei" et "affectus credulitatis" pour les Sémipelagiens?' in *Rech. sc. rel.* 35 (1948) 566-88.

[36] Matt. 15. 13.

[37] *voluntas spiritualis*, the spiritual or spiritualized will, the highest of the three degrees at which the human will can arrive; it is spiritualized by its union with the Spirit of God, or supernaturalized by grace.

[38] 1 Cor. 6. 17.

[39] The one end for which man is to act is God's glory. Only thanks to grace he is able to strive after this. Compare the Augustinian and Thomistic teaching that without grace fallen man is not able to love God above all things. Cf. St. Augustine, *Epist.* 217 (*Ad Vital.*) 12, 'Liberum arbitrium ad diligendum Deum primi peccati granditate perdidimus'; St. Thomas, *Sum. theol.* I. II. 109. 3.

[40] Cf. Augustine, *De spir. et litt.* 34. 60: 'Ac per hoc quid habeat et quid accipiat, Dei est: accipere autem et habere utique accipientis et habentis est.' God's gift remains His, but its acceptance is the inalienable role of man's free will. Cf. X. Léon-Dufour, 'Grâce et libre arbitre chez saint Augustin,' *Rech. sc. rel.* 33 (1946) 129-63, esp. 143-5.

[41] The question here asked concerns the process of justification or conversion: What happens in man when he is converted to God? The answer depends on the conception of the Fall: What did the deterioration of human nature through the first sin consist in?— The question is asked here in order to bring out the difference between the natural will (of chs. 4-6) that is not spiritualized by divine grace, and the spiritual will (of chs. 6 f.).

⁴² This picture of fallen man's state is Augustinian and to be understood in the Augustinian context: e.g. *voluntate captiva* (cf. *Epist.* 217 [*Ad Vital.*] 3. 8, *arbitrium captivum*)—the enslavement of the will is not the loss of its freedom but of its capacity to do good. As this chapter further explains, this whole corruption is *accidental,* leaving the substance of the nature untouched, though weakened or ill.

⁴³ Cf. above, ch. 4 nn. 16, 17; also 34.

⁴⁴ This conception of the effects of the Fall, according to which man has not changed the 'substance' of his will but lost only its integrity or soundness (which is righteousness), is derived from St. Augustine: cf. the following note. Compare *Carm. de ingr.* 581-92; *Contra coll.* 12. 4.

⁴⁵ *qualitate facta est mala*: man's nature which was good before sin, has turned bad accidentally, infected by an evil quality; but the substance of his will remains good. Cf. St. Augustine, *De perf. iust. hom.* 2. 4, 'qualitas secundum quam malus est animus.' This evil quality is remedied in justification—cf. Prosper, *Contra coll.* 18. 3, 'qualitate et conditione mutata per Mediatorem.'

⁴⁶ Ps. 77. 39.

⁴⁷ The catholic idea holds that the initiative of a conversion comes from God and not from man. Cassian taught the opposite, at least for some cases; *Coll.* 13.8, '. . . incrementum tribuens ei quem vel ipse plantavit vel *nostro conatu* viderit emersisse.'

⁴⁸ Compare St. Paul, 2 Cor. 5. 17 and Gal. 6. 15.

⁴⁹ Cf. *Contra coll.* 12. 4. Prosper's insistence on man's collaboration with grace is to be noted, and contrasted, with St. Augustine's exposition in *De spir. et litt.* 30.52.

⁵⁰ 1 John 3. 8.

⁵¹ Cf. *Contra coll.* 12, 'non est ab ipso quamvis non sine ipso conversio.'

⁵² Again, the initiative for a conversion comes from grace; cf. above, n. 47.

⁵³ Cf. Rom. 8. 14.

⁵⁴ Grace does not destroy freedom but heals and restores it. Cf. *Carm. de ingr.* 593 ff. The idea comes from St. Augustine (cf., e.g. *De pecc. mer.* 2. 17. 26—'ut suave fiat quod non delectabat, gratiae Dei est'). St. Prosper explains it in his own way. Cf. Cappuyns, 'L'auteur' 211 n. 2.

⁵⁵ B *ereptum,* M *interfectum.*

⁵⁶ The idea here is not clear. Girard translates (13): 'entre les

mains de qui rien n'est pery de ce qu'a perdu la Nature.' Mangeant refers to *Contra coll.* 12 ('. . . manens enim liberum arbitrium . . .'). This may be meant: God's favour, the source of grace, remained unchanged when nature lost grace.

[57] . . . *totumque quod virtus est, Deus est*: 'all that is virtue is God.' Cf. *Contra coll.* 13. 1: 'Virtus namque principaliter Deus est: cui non aliud est habere virtutem, quam esse virtutem.' Girard interprets, 'tout ce qui est de loüable en la vertu, est en Dieu.' The Ballerini remark, 'omnis virtus a Deo operante manat.'

[58] No true virtue without divine grace: cf. above, ch. 7.

[59] Isa. 43. 11.

[60] Jer. 10. 23.

[61] Cf. above, n. 52.

[62] Luke 12. 49.

[63] Cf. above, ch. 4.

[64] Cf. above, ch. 5.

[65] 1 Cor. 1. 21.

[66] The reason why the initiative in the process of a conversion comes from grace and not from man's free will, is mainly drawn here, as in St. Augustine, from the healing character of grace, for fallen nature is in dire need of a healing. The 'raising' character of grace, though not neglected, is left in the background.

[67] Cf. Matt. 11. 11 (Mark 7. 28); for the following, John 1. 9. The same idea about St. John the Baptist is found in St. Augustine, *De spir. et litt.* 7. 11.

[68] The Pelagian position admitted an exterior grace, the exterior preaching of the doctrine, as a necessary help to stir the human will, but denied that an interior grace or motion by God was needed. This error is here aimed at. Cf. also *Carm. de ingr.* 335-47; St. Augustine, *De grat. Christi* 1. 7-14; *De civ. Dei* 15. 6.

[69] The Law commands but does not give the strength to fulfill the commandment: cf. St. Paul, Rom. 7. St. Augustine in his *De spir. et litt.* develops this opposition between the Law and grace.

[70] Cf. Matt. 5. 17, and Augustine, *Enchir.* 1. 8. 20.

[71] Grace destroys sin through forgiveness without exacting the punishment laid down for the offence by the Law. This is shown in the example of Christ who did not condemn the adulterous woman (John 8. 1-11).

[72] Luke 19. 10.

[73] John 8. 6.

[74] Cf. St. Augustine's comment on this episode in *In Ioan. Ev. tract.* 23. 4-6; also *Serm.* 13. 4 f.

[75] Jer. 31. 33.

[76] *stylo Spiritus Sancti.* The idea expressed is that grace works interiorly in the human soul; the teaching of the Law was only an exterior help.

[77] Compare this description of the intimate action of grace in the soul with St. Augustine, *De civ. Dei* 15.6.

[78] Cf. above, ch. 2, the three levels or degrees of the human will. Through grace man passes from the natural to the spiritual will.

[79] . . . *ut lex peccati et lex Dei diversas et distinctas habeant mansiones*: the law of sin which rules the natural will, cannot be in the same way and at the same time in one man with the law of God that rules the spiritual will.

[80] Cf. Gal. 5. 17.

[81] A Pauline and Augustinian idea: the usefulness of temptation and trial for humility. This text is quoted by Pope Gelasius in his pamphlet against the Pelagians, ML 159. 127. Compare Trent's teaching on concupiscence 'quae ad agonem relicta sit' (ES 792).

[82] 2 Cor. 12. 7-9.

[83] His image—cf. Gen. 1. 27; the lost sheep—Luke 15. 5.

[84] Job 14. 4.

[85] Gal. 1. 22-24.

[86] Cf. Acts 4. 32.

[87] Cf., e.g. Acts 21. 19 f.

[88] Matt. 5. 16.

[89] Every good conducive to heaven, that is, all true virtue, ɔmes from grace in its beginning, its increase, and its permanence ɔr perseverance. The Semi-Pelagians denied the necessity of grace for the first and third of these stages.

[90] Cf. ch. 1 and n. 4.

[91] Cf. Phil. 3. 15 f.; St. Augustine, *De praed. sanct.* 1. 2.

[92] The passage between brackets is given by B (but bracketed also) and (also by Hurter) from Ms. *Vat. Lat.* 262. It is absent from M and also from the text in ML 17. Girard's translation does not include it either.

[93] *sacramenta vitae*—the sacraments of baptism, confirmation, and the Eucharist, received together by the catechumen at Easter. Cf. L. Duchesne, *Origines du culte chrétien* (5th ed. Paris 1925) ch. 9: 'L'initiation chrétienne.' The author states that those who became Christians but afterwards fell away from the faith, merely

'seemed' (*videbantur*) to come to these *life-giving* (*vitae*) sacraments. They never were among the elect. Cf. Augustine, *De corr. et grat.* 7. 16; 9. 20; 12. 36 ('qui autem cadunt et pereunt, in praedestinatorum numero non fuerunt'); *De dono persev.* 9. 21.

94 1 John 2. 19.

95 Titus 1. 16.

96 Rom. 10. 13.

97 Matt. 7. 21.

98 *Ibid.* 7. 22 f.

99 Rom. 8. 15.

100 1 Cor. 12. 3.

101 Rom. 8. 14.

102 1 Peter 2. 9.

103 *praesciti et praeordinati:* the 'foreknown and foreordained,' that is, the predestined. As noted in the Introduction (18), the term '*praedestinati*' is avoided. Girard translates *praeordinati* by *prédestiné*, but as if the text were a Scripture quotation from Rom. 4.

104 Jer. 31. 31-34. Compare St. Augustine, *De spir. et litt.* 24. 39 f.

105 Jer. 32. 39-41.

106 Isa. 43. 19-21.

107 *Ibid.* 45. 23 f.

108 The elect are infallibly saved because the election necessarily has its effect. This idea, though not different from St. Augustine's predestination, is not termed so. Cf. St. Augustine, *De corr. et grat.* 7. 13 f.

109 Prosper refers to the interior action of grace, stressed anew in opposition to the Pelagian idea of an exterior grace. Cf. above, n. 68.

110 1 Cor. 3. 7.

111 Cf. Jer. 31. 34.

112 B *custodiantur*, M *erudiantur*; Girard (22), 'qui leur fait garder ses commandements.'

113 Cf. Isa. 43. 19-21.

114 B *inundati*, M *mundati*.

115 Gal. 3. 15.

116 Namely, the salvation of the elect.

117 Rom. 3. 3 f.

118 Gen. 28. 14. Those who do not come to the faith after having it preached to them, never were among the elect, while the elect infallibly reach salvation. Cf. above, n. 108.

[119] Jer. 31. 34. A similar procedure in quoting Scripture texts is found in St. Augustine, *De spir. et litt.* 30. 52.

[120] Jer. *ibid.*

[121] *Ibid.* 32. 39.

[122] *Ibid.* 32. 40 f.

[123] B *credituros* (added from *Vat. Reg.* 293) *promisit,* M *promisit.*

[124] Isa. 45. 23 f.

[125] The difficulty, that in spite of God's promise to save all men, many are still outside the way to salvation, will be answered here by a restrictive interpretation of the salvific will. All men means, all the elect. Cf. *Resp. cap. Gall.* 13.

[126] *secundum illam incommutabilem scientiam*—the election is mainly considered as God's infallible foreknowledge of the elect.

[127] Prosper's exegesis here and in the following may appear somewhat artificial or clumsy. It is inspired by a preconceived idea about the salvific will which he learned from Augustine's restrictive interpretations of Scripture. Here, in accounting for the number of those that are *actually* saved, the Augustinian idea of *specialis universitas,* a restricted totality, is applied. See below, n. 137.

[128] 2 Cor. 5. 17.

[129] Col. 1. 19 f.

[130] Heb. 1. 2.

[131] Ps. 2. 8.

[132] John 12. 32.

[133] Isa. 40. 4.

[134] *Ibid.* 66. 23.

[135] Joel 2. 28.

[136] Ps. 144. 14.

[137] *specialis universitas*: a specified totality (cf. B's marginal note: '*plenitudo universitas electorum*'). The elect are taken from all over the world and for that reason the whole world is said to be saved. They constitute a totality, but specified or restricted. See St. Augustine's interpretation of 1 Tim. 2. 4 in *Enchir.* 27. 103 (cf. also L. A. Arand's remarks in ACW 3. 141 n. 336): 'Per omnes homines omne genus humanum intelligamus per quascumque differentias distributum'; or *De corr. et grat.* 14. 44: 'Ita dictum est omnes homines salvos fieri, ut intelligantur omnes praedestinati; quia omne genus hominum in iis est.' This is, moreover, a common way of speaking. We say, 'All nations were present,' 'The whole of Europe or America thinks like that,' when there are some rep-

resentatives of all these nations or countries who came or are of that opinion.

[138] . . . *ut de toto mundo totus mundus liberatus et de omnibus hominibus omnes homines videantur assumpti*: the elect are chosen from all over the world and thus the whole world is said to have been liberated; they are taken from among all mankind and so the whole of mankind is said to have been chosen. Cf. Girard (25): '. . . une certaine plénitude, comme si un monde estoit séparé d'un autre monde, ou si tous les hommes estoient choisis d'entre tous les autres hommes.'

[139] The argument *a pari* taken from the texts concerning the reprobate will seem weak. Replaced in their context these quotations do not mean to say a totality or universality. The author is aware of it; cf. below, n. 144.

[140] John 3. 31 f.

[141] Phil. 2. 21.

[142] Ps. 13. 2 f.

[143] It is hard for us to see the importance of an argumentation built on a figure of speech (called hyperbole).

[144] The context itself of the Scripture texts indicates what is meant by an apparently universalistic expression.

[145] 1 Cor. 1. 23 f.

[146] Girard seems to misunderstand when he translates (27): 'il a compris les fidelles et les infidelles sous le nom général des appelés.'

[147] . . . *vocationis extraneos*: a discreet way of expressing reprobation. Cf. Intro. n. 49, on St. Prosper's conception of the reprobation '*post praevisa merita.*'

[148] This chapter builds an argument on another stylistic figure, called in rhetoric 'metonymy of the part for the whole.' A whole is named to designate now one part of it and then another; e.g. man is mortal—that is, his body is mortal; man does not die, that is, his soul does not die.

[149] B *hanc regulam*, M *hac regula.*

[150] Isa. 42. 16.

[151] *Ibid.* 42. 17.

[152] *Ibid.* 43. 5-7.

[153] *Ibid.* 43. 8.

[154] *reliquiae*: cf. Rom. 11. 5, cited below, *reliquiae secundum electionem gratiae*—'a remnant saved according to the election of grace.' In spite of many going astray, grace always chose a rem-

nant of the people to itself. This remainder is reckoned as a totality: see the same idea above (n. 137)—*specialis universitas*. Cf. St. Augustine, *De dono persev.* 18. 47. For this 'remainder' of Israel, cf. L. Cerfaux, *La théologie de l'Eglise suivant Saint Paul* (Paris 1942) 115 f.

155 Rom. 11. 1 f.

156 *sibi reliquos fecit:* lit. 'made them into its remnant or remainder'; see above, n. 154.

157 M inserts *inquit,* B omits this.

158 Rom. 11. 2-6. Cf. M. J. Lagrange, *Saint Paul, Epître aux Romains* (5th M Paris 1931) 270; J. Sickenberger, *Die Briefe des heiligen Paulus an die Korinther und Römer* (4th ed. Bonn 1932) 262 f.

159 . . . *partem sibi illuminatio gratuita reservavit:* grace kept the other section of the people of Israel as its remnant—the *reliquiae* of Rom. 11 just cited (n. 154).

160 Rom. 11. 28. Cf. the same reasoning on this text in St. Augustine, *De praed. sanct.* 16. 33.

161 Rom. 11. 25.

162 The whole gist of this chapter comes to this: the expression *all* at times designates a totality, at times one section of this totality, at other times still another section of the same. The context indicates which of the three possible meanings applies in each case. The intention of this whole discussion is evidently to show that even a restricted interpretation of the divine salvific will would not go counter to the meaning of the Scriptural texts, since other examples of a similar usage abound.

163 Introducing one more study of a figure of speech or a way of speaking which has little direct relation with the question of the universal salvific will, but is meant to stress the need of understanding or interpreting some statements of Scripture.

164 1 Peter 2. 9 f.

165 Acts 14. 15.

166 B *vocabuntur,* M *vocabantur.*

167 *loquendi consuetudo,* usage in speaking, which is common parlance and not particular to Scripture.

168 *prope mundi finem,* towards the end of the world. The idea implied is that Christ's coming has inaugurated the last world period. As to how St. Augustine understood this, cf. *Epist.* 199 (*Ad Hesych.*) 6. 17. See also J. P. Christopher, ACW 2. 136 nn. 250 f.

169 The figure of speech on which the argument in this chapter

is built is called metonymy of the effect or substitution of the effect (here, the descendants) for the cause (the forefathers).

[170] . . . *qui amant calumniosa certamina,* sophistical or slanderous wranglings, meant for the Semi-Pelagians; cf. *Resp. cap. Gall.* 1 and *Resp. cap. Vincent.* 1.

[171] 1 Tim. 2. 4. After the long discussions on hermeneutics in the three preceding chapters, the author comes to his point, as to how to interpret this text in St. Paul.

[172] Perhaps there is some truth in the objection. It is hard to reconcile—and it may be questioned whether St. Prosper here or in his previous works succeeds in doing so—a particularist conception of the real salvific will, or of the election and predestination, with St. Paul's text. Our author claims to do so. He himself may have sensed something of the incoherence or lack of synthesis in his own teaching, as is pointed out by Amann, *art. cit.* 1832. Cf. Intro. n. 56.

[173] 1 Tim. 2. 1-6.

[174] . . . *hac ergo doctrinae apostolicae regula . . . imbuitur.*

[175] *si obedientia concordat in studio,* if obedience to the command leads to agreement in action. Cf. Girard (32), 'la loi ne pourra estre douteuse, si l'on demeure d'accord de l'obéissance qui lui est deüe.'

[176] Cf. a similar interpretation in *Resp. cap. Vincent.* 2; *Contra coll.* 12; also in St. Augustine, *Enchir.* 27. 103; cf. *De corr. et grat.* 15. 47, 'nos facit velle.'

[177] *sancti,* in the sense of St. Paul (e.g. Eph. 3. 8) =Christians. Cf. H. Delehaye, *Sanctus* (Brussels 1927) esp. 24-59.

[178] This text (see also below, Book Two, ch. 37) is quite reminiscent of the solemn prayers chanted after the singing of the Passion on Good Friday, and it is given here in the Latin: 'Supplicat ergo ubique Ecclesia Deo, non solum pro sanctis et in Christo regeneratis, sed etiam pro omnibus infidelibus et inimicis crucis Christi, pro omnibus idolorum cultoribus, pro omnibus qui Christum in membris ipsius persequuntur, pro Iudaeis quorum caecitati lumen Evangelii non refulget, pro haereticis et schismaticis, qui ab unitate fidei et caritatis alieni sunt.' The so-called *orationes solemnes* of Good Friday appear to be a remnant of the ancient 'prayer of the faithful' (*oratio fidelium*) regularly recited in the Mass of the Roman liturgy after the sermon or homily and before the offertory. Cf. Duchesne, *op. cit.* 182 f.; esp. V. L. Kennedy,

*The Saints of the Canon of the Mass* (Studi di antichità cristiana 14, Rome 1938) 31 f., where the present passage is noticed.

[179] Contrast this with Prosper's criticism of the idea of a universal salvific will in his *Epist. ad Ruf. 13.*

[180] This chapter meets the classical objection against the given interpretation of 1 Tim. 2. 4; it does not solve, but only shifts, the crux of the problem.

[181] The answer to the objection is that we do not know the reasons of God's mysterious decrees which rule the dispensation of graces, and St. Paul's example in the matter is referred to. Cf. St. Augustine in *De spir. et litt.* 34. 60. On the fideistic or agnostic aspect of this renouncement of knowledge, cf. X. Léon-Dufour, *art. cit.* 160. At its basis is an anthropomorphic transposition into God of human freedom of choice, thus establishing in God a choice between the elect and the reprobate.

[182] 1 Cor. 13. 9.

[183] *Ibid.* 13. 12.

[184] A conflation by St. Paul, quoting from memory, of Isa. 59. 20 f. and 27. 9.

[185] Rom. 11. 25-32. Cf. St. Augustine's similar reflexion on this text in *De grat. et lib. arb.* 22. 44.

[186] Girard translates (35): 'Il ne donne pour toute raison de l'exposition qu'il avoit faite, qu'un enthousiasme qui le fit écrier comme un homme ravy en extase.'

[187] Rom. 11. 33-36. Cf. St. Augustine, *Contra duas epist. Pelag.* 4. 6. 16; or *Serm.* 17. 6 f.

[188] St. Prosper is alive to the problems involved in the mysterious economy of men's salvation, particularly in the historical development or unfolding of this divine plan with regard to Israel and the Gentiles. According to St. Paul this comprises three stages: 1) the election of Israel and the abandonment of the nations; 2) the unbelief of the chosen people who rejected the Messias and the conversion of the nations; 3) after the conversion of the Gentiles, the return of Israel. St. Paul says that the reason of this economy of graces has not been made known to men. Cf. F. Prat, *The Theology of St. Paul* (tr. by J. Stoddard, London 1945) 1. 249-67. For present-day controversies on this teaching of St. Paul, cf. G. Fessard, 'Théologie et histoire, à propos du temps de la conversion d'Israël,' *Dieu Vivant* 8 (1947) 37-65.

[189] Cf. Acts 14. 15.

[190] Rom. 11. 25.

191 The principle of a solution for these last two questions has been given in chs. 9 and 10; *all* signifies a restricted or specified totality.

192 This blind trust in the wisdom of God's revelation which teaches us all that we need to know, so that what has not been revealed we need not know, is found elsewhere in St. Prosper: cf. *Epist. ad Ruf.* 13, 'sine fidei diminutione nescitur'; *Carm. de ingr.* 752 f.

193 This chapter intends to justify the author's answer to the problems raised by his interpretation of 1 Tim. 2. 4 (which was that we do not know the reason of God's dispositions), by enlarging the issue, and showing that many other things remain mysterious to us in the divine world economy.

194 According to the Christian conception, God's Providence is the cause of all inequalities among men and among creatures in general. This does not, as we know, exclude as executing agents of Providence the secondary or created causes.

195 Pagan fatalism of the Romans held that all events are unalterably predetermined by the blind power personified in the goddesses of destiny. Cf. St. Augustine, *De civ. Dei* 5. 8; St. Prosper, *Resp. cap. Gall.* 1, 'Fati enim opinio vana est, et de falsitate concepta.'

196 Astrology believed in the occult influence of the stars upon human affairs, particularly upon the destiny and character of individual men said to be dependent on the constellation under which they are born. Cf. on ancient astrology, A. J. Festugière, *La révélation d'Hermes Trismégiste* I: *L'astrologie et les sciences occultes* (Paris 1944). Cf. also St. Augustine, *De civ. Dei* 5. 1-7.

197 Bodies are of one nature, made out of the four elements, according to the philosophy of the time; souls are of one nature, spirits created by God. The differences in the individual men come from different proportions in which both are adjusted to each other: cf. *Carm. de ingr.* 728 f. Compare St. Augustine, *De div. quaest.* 83. 40; *Opus imp. c. Iul.* 4. 128; *De Gen. ad litt.* 10. 17. 30.

198 Cf. *Epist. ad Ruf.* 13; *Resp. excerp. Gen.* 8; also Augustine, *De praed. sanct.* 8. 16; *De dono persev.* 11. 27.

199 Exod. 4. 11.

200 Isa. 66. 9. B *Nonne ecce ego*, M *Nonne ego*.

201 Ecclus. 11. 14.

202 Job 12. 6.

[203] *Ibid.* 12. 13-25.

[204] *Ibid.* 23. 15.

[205] In ch. 15 begin the proofs for the gratuitousness of grace; at the same time stress is laid on the need of discerning between what is hidden from our knowledge and what has been revealed to us about the salvation of mankind.

[206] The first proof for the gratuitousness of grace is drawn from the fact that so many nations in the past ages have not been called to the true religion whilst their descendants who were not better that their own ancestors, have been. Cf. Prosper, *Epist. ad Aug.* 5.

[207] Isa. 9. 2.

[208] 1 Peter 2. 9 f.

[209] *minores et maiores,* the descendants and the ancestors.

[210] Cf. above, n. 192; *Carm. de ingr.* 709-11. See also Augustine, *De civ. Dei,* 12. 27. 2–'. . . occulto Dei iudicio, sed tamen iusto'; *Opus imp. c. Iul.* 1. 48.

[211] Another proof for the gratuitousness of grace is the case of infants who die without baptism. Cf. *Epist. ad Aug.* 5; *Epist. ad Ruf.* 7; *Carm. de ingr.* 616-28; and St. Augustine, *De grat. et lib. arb.* 22. 44; *De praed. sanct.* 12. 24; *De dono persev.* 9. 21 f.; *Epist.* 194 (*Ad Sixt.*) 7. 32.

[212] St. Augustine speaks of the *mitissima damnatio* of unbaptized infants: cf. *Enchir.* 23. 93 (ACW 3. 88 and n. 301). St. Prosper still holds on to this conception which to-day has been considerably mitigated. Cf., e.g. A. Gaudel, '*Limbes,*' DTC 9 .1 (1926) 760-72.

[213] Compare the Semi-Pelagian solution of the case of the infants as reported to Augustine by Prosper in his *Epist. ad Aug.* 5, or by Hilary in his own *Epist. ad Aug.* 8, that, namely, infants die with or without baptism according to God's foreknowledge of the merit or demerit they would have gained *if* they had been allowed to attain adult age. St. Augustine's answer is given in *De praed. sanct.* 12-14, 23-29; and earlier in *Contra duas epist. Pelag.* 2. 7. 14; also *Epist.* 194 (*Ad Sixt.*) 8.35 and 9. 41 f.

[214] Side by side with the argument for the gratuitousness of grace in these chs. 15-18 is the insistence on the necessity of discerning between the known and the unknown elements in God's economy of grace. The facts we see, the motives we cannot know.

[215] Regarding this third proof for the gratuitousness of grace and of the unknowability of God's mysterious designs—deathbed conversions—cf. also *Epist. ad Ruf.* 17, and *Carm. de ingr.* 434-8.

[216] The gratuitousness of grace refers to both merit and demerit;

sinful works cannot prevent grace, and good works cannot claim it as their reward.

[217] As the Semi-Pelagians held, namely, that grace waits for our good will (sometimes, if not always). Cf. above, n. 9.

[218] This is not to be understood as if innocence and sin were the same thing, but in such wise that natural merit has no better claim on grace than sinfulness. The parity of the just and the sinners expressed here refers to original sin in which all are born and which includes all in the *massa damnationis*, the Augustinian idea of the first sin according to which God's justice could rightly condemn all men for all eternity because of this original guilt; His mercy, however, chooses out of this condemned multitude His own elect. Cf. *De civ. Dei* 21. 12.

[219] The divine justice, so repeatedly stressed here, implies that God decrees nothing arbitrarily, but everything for some good reason often unknown to us. Cf. St. Augustine, *De grat. et. lib. arb.* 21. 43 (referring to Rom. 9. 14).

[220] God's free decrees we cannot know except after the event, or through revelation.

[221] Cf. *Resp. cap. Vincent.* 2, '. . . de quo dici non potest, aliter eum quidquam facere debuisse quam fecerit.'

[222] Cf. Matt. 20. 1-16; Augustine, *De dono persev.* 7. 17.–M inserts here between brackets, 'quo vitae aeternae significatur aequalitas,' which is found in one MS and the early editors and which Quesnel (cf. n. in M *ad loc.*) regarded as an interpolation reflecting the opinion of the heretic Jovinian, a contemporary of St. Jerome. On the interpretation of the parable, see M. J. Lagrange, *Evangile selon saint Matthieu* (8th ed. Paris 1948) 384-6.

[223] Matt. 20. 13-15.

[224] Perhaps not only to him! The absolute gratuitousness of grace is an idea of which it is difficult to grasp the import and implications. Pelagius had insisted on the fact that God is not 'gratiosus aut personarum acceptor' (cf. Plinval, *op. cit.* 230), implying and saying that He gives equal chances to all men, '. . . cum universa turba credentium paria dona gratiae percipiat' (Plinval, *ibid.*). Against this, cf. St. Augustine, *Epist. 186* (*Ad Paulin.*) 6. 16.

[225] Girard mistranslates *volentis potestas*, 'le pouvoir du Franc-Arbitre.'

[226] Rom. 9. 20.

[227] Here follows the conclusion of the preceding chs. 15-17 on the gratuitousness of grace. Pelagius had held 'gratiam Dei secun-

dum merita nostra dari' (cf. Augustine, *De grat. Christi* 1. 22. 23).
Our author will show, ch. 22, that the Semi-Pelagians, when ascribing the *initium fidei* to man's free will and not to grace, logically
hold on to the Pelagian error.

228 John 3. 5.

229 *Ibid.* 6. 54.

230 Referring to the exterior grace of Pelagius, the hearing of the
Law or of the doctrine; cf. above, n. 76.

231 Cf. ch. 6 and n. 34.

232 Both B and M discard Quesnel's reading *quae* (=the virtues)
in place of *qui.*

233 Cf. above, ch. 4 and nn. 16 f.

234 Cf. Gal. 3. 22.

235 Eph. 2. 1-3.

236 *Ibid.* 2. 12.

237 *Ibid.* 5. 8.

238 Col. 1. 12 f.

239 Titus 3. 3-7.

240 Confirmation of the preceding doctrine on the gratuitousness
of grace: nature without grace is but corruption and error; how
could it merit grace? Cf. St. Augustine, *Contra duas epist. Pelag.*
2. 5. 9.

241 Jude 10.

242 Luke 1. 76-79.

243 After the discussion on the gratuitousness of grace in the
preceding chapters, meant to explain partly why the grace that
saves does not reach all men, the idea of the universality of God's
calling is taken up again, to answer other difficulties against it.
In the present chapter two series of Scriptural texts confront each
other: one shows Christ's call to all men, the other asserts that
men refuse to answer His call. The synthesis of both, according to
the *De vocatione,* is given by the salvation of the elect; this constitutes the actual fulfilment of God's call.

244 John 11. 51 f.

245 Matt. 11. 25 f., 27, 28-30.

246 John 3. 31-33.

247 *Ibid.* 1. 10.

248 *Ibid.* 1. 5.

249 *Ibid.* 3. 31 f.

250 *Ibid.* 11. 52.

251 Matt. 11. 25.

<sup>252</sup> Cf. Luke 10. 22.

<sup>253</sup> Cf. Rom. 9. 24.

<sup>254</sup> *Ibid.* 4. 20 f.

<sup>255</sup> 1 John 5. 19 f. We could summarize this chapter in the three logical moments: thesis, God calls all men; antithesis, men refuse His call; synthesis, God saves His elect.

<sup>256</sup> The election of Israel and non-election of the Gentiles is a classical proof of the gratuitousness of grace, as also of the inscrutability of God's designs. The first aspect of this mystery was treated above, ch. 13. The second is considered here.

<sup>257</sup> In Book Two, especially in chs. 4, 19, 23, and 25, Prosper will explain how a general grace (cf. above, n. 27) is given to all men, no one excepted.

<sup>258</sup> As noted already (above, n. 4), the *De vocatione* insists on distinguishing between what we can know and what we cannot know: cf. Book Two, ch. 1.

<sup>259</sup> The Pelagians explained away the mystery of predestination, and the Semi-Pelagians found in the initiative of man's will the reason why grace is given or not given.

<sup>260</sup> Gal. 1. 1.

<sup>261</sup> Cf. ch. 14.

<sup>262</sup> Rom. 11. 32.

<sup>263</sup> On the three historical stages in the economy of man's salvation, see above, ch. 13 and n. 188.

<sup>264</sup> Obviously directed against the Semi-Pelagians and their *calumniosa certamina* of ch. 12.

<sup>265</sup> B *alios elegit, aliosque non elegit,* M *alios eligit, aliosque non eligit.* B remark that when speaking of the divine election the past tense is used in Scripture and ordinary usage.

<sup>266</sup> Matt. 20. 16.

<sup>267</sup> The Semi-Pelagian position as understood by St. Prosper— cf. *Epist. ad Aug.* 4: '. . . bono naturae bene usus ad istam salvantem gratiam initialis gratiae ope meruerit pervenire'; *Contra coll.* 20.

<sup>268</sup> B *diffinitio,* M *definitio,* in the sense of opinion or statement; cf. *Contra coll.* 19.

<sup>269</sup> . . . *ut interim de gratiae veritate taceatur,* as already argued in chapter 1; if grace is given for merit, and not gratuitously, it is no longer grace but something due to man. Cf. St. Augustine, *De gest. Pelag.* 14. 33: 'Ipsum quippe gratiae nomen, et eius nominis intellectus aufertur, si non gratis datur, sed eam qui dignus est accipit.'

270 The case of infants has already been considered above, ch. 16, as a proof of the gratuitousness of grace. Here it is taken as an argument against the Semi-Pelagian conception that merit is the reason for discrimination between the elect and the non-elect or reprobate. In infants there can be no question of merit. Cf. the same reasoning in St. Augustine, *De praed. sanct.* 12. 23.

271 Job 12. 10.

272 *Ibid.* 14. 5.

273 St. Prosper corners the Semi-Pelagians by a dilemma: Either you attribute the discrimination between infants, baptised and saved, or unbaptised and lost, to chance—which would be to fall into pagan fatalism (cf. above, n. 195); or you assert that there is no real discrimination of the infants, as the unbaptised are not lost, which supposes that they are without original sin—and this is Pelagianism. Even the Pelagians rejected pagan fatalism (cf. St. Augustine, *Epist.* 194 [*Ad Sixt.*] 7. 31); but their denial of original sin was condemned by the Church (cf. the foll. n.). It is interesting to remember that according to St. Prosper (*Epist. ad Aug.* 3) fatalism is exactly the objection made against St. Augustine's doctrine of predestination. Augustine himself had repudiated this interpretation, *Contra duas epist. Pelag.* 2. 5. 9; and retorted the accusation of fatalism against the Pelagians themselves: *ibid.* 2. 6. 11.—As noted already, the Semi-Pelagians did give an argument for the discrimination of infants, namely, their 'futurible' merits; a sophism which was answered by St. Augustine (cf. above, n. 213).

274 In the General Council of Africa, the Sixteenth of Carthage, of the year 418: cf. Mansi 3. 811; Hefele-Leclercq 2. 1. 192 = ES 102.

275 Luke 19. 10.

276 Some of their arguments may be found in *Contra coll.* 7.

277 B *omnibus hominibus*, M *omnibus*.

278 This refers to the Scripture examples which follow in the chapter, not to what precedes.

279 In the preceding chapter St. Prosper has shown that the Semi-Pelagian teaching about the case of infants is erroneous. Here he will refute their theories about the justification or call to the faith of adults. Let it be recalled that their two chief unorthodox tenets are these: the beginning of the faith and final perseverance are due to man's free will, not to grace. This ch. 23 refutes the first from the Scriptures.

[280] The accumulated Scripture texts not only refute the Semi-Pelagian position just mentioned, but also prove that all good in man is due to grace. This stresses once more the absolute gratuitousness of grace—one of the elements in the solution proposed by the *De vocatione* of the problem it studies, namely, the salvation of mankind.

[281] Rom. 1. 8.

[282] Eph. 1. 15-18.

[283] Col. 1. 3-5.

[284] *Ibid.* 1. 9-11.

[285] 1 Thess. 1. 2 f.

[286] *Ibid.* 2. 13.

[287] 2 Thess. 1. 3-5.

[288] 1 Peter 1. 18-21.

[289] 2 Peter 1. 1.

[290] 1 John 4. 2 f.

[291] *Ibid.* 4. 6.

[292] Acts 3. 16.

[293] *Ibid.* 16. 13 f.

[294] Matt. 16. 15-17.

[295] Rom. 12. 3.

[296] *Ibid.* 15. 5 f.

[297] *Ibid.* 15. 13.

[298] Eph. 2. 4-6, 8-10.

[298a] Cf. 1 Cor. 3. 9.

[299] The preceding chapter has proved that the beginning of all good, *initium fidei,* is due to grace. It remains to be shown that faith is the source of all good and virtuous work. By faith is meant here the 'fides quae per caritatem operatur': cf. Gal. 5. 6.

[300] B *conferantur,* M *consequantur.*

[301] Ps. 36. 23 f.

[302] *Ibid.* 42. 3.

[303] *Ibid.* 58. 10 f.

[304] Prov. 2. 6 (Sept.).

[305] *Ibid.* 8. 14-16 (Sept.).

[306] *Ibid.* 20. 24 (Sept.); B *a Domino diriguntur,* M *corriguntur.*

[307] *Ibid.* 21. 2 (Sept.).

[308] *Ibid.* 8. 35 (Sept.).

[309] *Ibid.* 19. 21 (Sept.).

[310] Eccles. 5. 17 f.

[311] *Ibid.* 8. 17-9. 1. B *universum hoc dedit,* M *dedi.*

[312] Wisd. 7. 15 f.

[313] *Ibid.* 8. 21.

[314] 1 Cor. 7. 7.

[315] Matt. 19. 10 f.

[316] Ecclus. 1. 22 f.

[317] *Ibid.* 25. 14 f.

[318] Isa. 33. 6 (Sept.).

[319] *Ibid.* 40. 12-14 (Sept.).

[320] Job 41. 2.

[321] Jer. 10. 23.

[322] *Ibid.* 24. 6 f.

[323] Bar. 2. 31.

[324] 1 Cor. 12. 3-11. B *gratia sanitatum in eodem Spiritu,* M *in uno Spiritu.*

[325] Eph. 4. 4-8.

[326] 2 Cor. 3. 4-6.

[327] *Ibid.* 9. 8-11.

[328] Eph. 3. 14-21.

[329] James 1. 16 f.

[330] Zach. 9. 16 f. (Sept.).

[331] Matt. 13. 10 f.

[332] John 3. 27.

[333] *Ibid.* 6. 44 f.

[334] *Ibid.* 6. 66.

[335] Phil. 1. 6.

[336] Cf. Girard (69), 'celui d'entre vous qui aura bien commencé, finira bien.'

[337] Cf. B's marginal note, 'Pelagiana interpretatio loci Paulini.' Prosper rather refers to the Semi-Pelagian position which claimed for man's free will both the beginning of faith and the completion of perseverance; see *Contra coll.* 19 (*quarta definitio*); in general, also Augustine, *De praed. sanct.* and *De dono persev.*—Cf. Pelagius' commentary: A. Souter, *Pelagius' Exposition of Thirteen Epistles of St. Paul* 2 (Cambridge 1926) 389.

[338] Phil. 1. 28 f.

[339] *Ibid.* 2. 12 f. B *sui operatur velle et operari,* M . . . *et perficere.*

[340] 1 Thess. 3. 11-13.

[341] 1 Cor. 1. 4-8. The phrase, '*proficientem perseverantiam,*' is Augustinian: *Epist.* 217 (*Ad Vital.*) 5; *De dono persev.* 20. 53.

[342] Rom. 8. 35-37.

[343] 1 Cor. 15. 56 f.

[344] 1 Thess. 5. 23 f.

[345] 2 Thess. 2. 15–3. 3.

[346] 1 Peter 5. 10 f.

[347] 1 John 4. 4.

[348] *Ibid.* 5. 4.

[349] Luke 22. 31 f., 46. B *et rogate,* M *et roga.* The old and new versions of the text are here combined, as also in *Epist. ad Ruf.* 10 and *Contra coll.* 15. 3.

[350] John 10. 26-28.

[351] *Ibid.* 6. 37-39.

[352] The concluding chapter of Book One repeats once more the principle that we cannot know the reasons of God's ruling in His dispensation of graces; which shows how the Semi-Pelagian attempt to solve the problem by calling in free will fails to give an explanation.

[353] 1 Cor. 4. 7. Cf. *Contra coll.* 13. 6.

[354] Cf. Rom. 11. 33-36.

[355] As the Semi-Pelagians tried to explain, according to St. Prosper's *Epist. ad Aug.* 4, '. . . ut et qui voluerint fiant filii Dei, et inexcusabiles sint qui fideles esse noluerint.' Cf. *Carm. de ingr.* 757 f.

[356] Cf. above, ch. 6: There is no real or true virtue without grace and without the true faith.

[357] Luke 19. 10.

[358] *illa pars fidei:* according to St. Prosper the universal salvific will is a doctrine of faith, and not a mere human theory.

[359] When we recall Cassian's insistence on the universal salvific will and the conclusion he drew from this doctrine, namely, that the initiative in the process of salvation belongs to free will, we shall not be surprised that Prosper in the *De vocatione* has devoted the entire first book to the study of the gratuitousness of grace. He must synthetise this doctrine with the universality of God's salvific will. This latter will chiefly be studied in Book Two. Cf. the Introduction 12 and n. 55. For Cassian, see *Coll. 13—De protectione divina* 7: 'Propositum namque Dei, quo non ob hoc hominem fecerat ut periret, sed ut in perpetuum viveret, manet immobile. Cuius benignitas cum bonae voluntatis in nobis quantulamcumque scintillam emicuisse perspexerit, vel quam ipse tamquam de dura silice cordis excuderit, confovet eam et exsuscitat, suaque inspiratione confortat, volens omnes homines salvos fieri et ad agnitionem veritatis venire. . . . Qui enim ut pereat unus ex pusillis non habet voluntatem, quomodo sine ingenti sacrilegio putandus est,

non universaliter omnes, sed quosdam salvos fieri velle pro omnibus?' From this he concludes: 'Praesto est ergo cotidie Christi gratia, quae, dum vult omnes homines salvos fieri et ad agnitionem veritatis venire, cunctos absque ulla exceptione convocat.' Grace is ready for all, but often, according to Cassian, waits for man's good will. Cf. Prosper, *Epist. ad Aug.* 4.

## BOOK TWO

[1] Book Two proposes to answer the following question: If many men are not saved, as is admitted and explained in Book One, how then can it be said that the divine salvific will is really universal? Cf. the Intro. 13 f.

[2] Cf. Book One, ch. 25 and n. 358: *pars fidei,* a doctrine of faith.

[3] B *agnitionem,* M *cognitionem.*

[4] Cf. Book One, ch. 23.

[5] Cf. Book One, chs. 14 and 21.

[6] Girard seems to translate a different reading (76), 'si la première ou la seconde Vérité nous est inconnüe.'

[7] Cf. Rom. 9. 14.

[8] Ps. 24. 10.

[9] That is, *iustitia et misericordia,* justice and mercy—cf. Book One, ch. 15; *Resp. cap. Vincent.* 2: 'Ut enim reus damnetur, inculpabilis Dei iustitia est; ut autem reus iustificetur, ineffabilis Dei gratia est.' Cf. also Augustine, *De dono persev.* 8. 17 f. Girard here apparently again translates a different text (76), 'et couronne ses dons quand il récompense les Justes.'

[10] Ps. 62. 12.

[11] *Ibid.* 50. 6.

[12] Ch. 2 states the doctrine of faith which is to be explained in the following chapters.

[13] This is not to be understood as excluding all *fides quaerens intellectum*; the whole purpose of the *De vocatione* aims at understanding the faith, and Book Two will propose an explanation of the problem connected with a mystery of the faith.

[14] Matt. 28. 18-20.

[15] Mark 16. 15.

[16] Matt. 28. 30.

[17] Cf. *ibid.* 10. 16.

[18] Cf. *ibid.* 3. 9.

[19] *Ibid.* 10. 17-22.

[20] Titus 2. 11.

[21] *plenitudinis censum fidelium*—cf. what was said about this *specialis universitas* in Book One, ch. 9 nn. 137 and 138.

[22] 1 John 2. 1 f.

[23] Ch. 3 begins the explanation of our problem by removing one difficulty: the divine call is delayed for some peoples.

[24] Mark. 16. 15.

[25] Matt. 10. 5 f.

[26] 1 Tim. 2. 4.

[27] God sees to it that all things happen according to His decrees and not differently.—Girard reads (80), '. . . donne un autre cours à sa Providence.'

[28] Acts 16. 6.

[29] Cf. *ibid.* 16. 7. The Scripture reminiscences here mix two versions: *vetiti sunt* is from the Vulgate, and *prohibiti sunt* from the older version; so, too, in *Contra coll.* 12.

[30] The mystery of man's salvation of which we know God's design (He wills all men to be saved) is brought out more wonderfully by the fact that the call of some men and some nations is delayed. The contrast of this element of obscurity in God's plan gives relief to the bright light of the salvific will. This is one of St. Prosper's own views and opinions (cf. Book One, ch. 1). Girard translates (80): 'afin que par l'interposition de quelques voiles, les Vérités les plus occultes paraissent à nos yeux avec plus d'éclat.'

[31] Cf. Mal. 4. 2.

[32] Cf. Wisd. 5. 6.

[33] Cf. Book One, ch. 12, the interpretation of 1 Tim. 2. 4, and ch. 13, the difficulty arising from that interpretation: Why does not God hear the prayers offered Him for all men?

[34] The solution of our problem is being prepared by pointing to a classical example of differences in the divine call to salvation: Israel was called with a special grace, all other men with a general one only. Cf. Book One, ch. 5 and nn. 28 and 29; also *Contra coll.* 7 and *Resp. cap. Gall.* 8. See St. Paul, Rom. 1 and 2.

[35] Cf. Ps. 76. 19.

[36] Cf. Acts 14. 15.

[37] *Ibid.* 32. 5.

[38] Ps. 118. 155.

[39] *Ibid.* 32. 5.

[40] . . . *per quae dona ac sacramenta.*

[41] Acts 14. 14-16. B *benefaciens eis,* M *benefaciens.*

[42] B *de bonitate ac potestate,* M *de bonitate.*

[43] B *innumerabilium beneficiorum,* M *inenarrabilium.*

[44] Cf. 2 Cor. 2. 16.

[45] Cf. *ibid.* 3. 6.—Would not this reference to the Scriptural text insinuate that in the conception of the *De vocatione* God's call to all nations through the medium of things created is not only an exterior teaching but also implies an interior action of His Spirit? Cf. the Ballerini's note, 'quatenus sine spiritu gratiae sola exteriora auxilia nequeunt plane erudire nec ad verum Dei cultum et amorem perducere.' This general grace would then truly involve a supernatural element. Cf. below, n. 226, on the *gratia generalis.—* St. Augustine, *De spir. et litt.* 14. 23, says, 'Decalogus occidit, nisi adsit gratia.' Prosper confirms this in the following chapter: the Gentiles who did profit of the testimony of things created did so thanks to an interior grace of faith. Compare the negative counterproof of ch. 4, Book One.

[46] Among the Jews also it was an interior grace, not the Law that justified the elect: see St. Paul, Rom. 2. 29 and 3. 30; and ch. 4, the example of Abraham's faith.

[47] The *De vocatione* takes for granted that some Gentiles have been able to please God and were enabled to do this by grace. They, therefore, received grace. This is consistent with the teaching of ch. 6, Book One: as long as the virtues of the infidels are not helped by grace, they are not true virtues. Here the possibility is admitted that infidels in the past have received grace. The admission is pregnant with far-reaching consequences for the salvation of the infidels. Cf. St. Augustine, *De civ. Dei* 18. 47, '. . . etiam per alias gentes esse potuisse qui secundum Deum vixerunt eique placuerunt.'

[48] *parcior*—grace was given more sparingly to the Gentiles than to the Jews—if only because of the lesser abundance of exterior means of grace. The pagans disposed of one source of knowledge of God only, the created things, not two (or more, cf. below, ch. 9) as did the Israelites who had besides the first, the Law and the Prophets.

[49] Grace is 'one in power,' equally able to gain the Gentiles and the Jews; 'varying in measure,' cf. the previous note and the following chapter; 'immutable in its design,' infallibly leading to

God's purpose in granting it—salvation (as in fact 'efficacious' grace does); 'multiform in its effects,' that is, there are different virtues in different degrees according to the different men to whom it is given.

⁵⁰ God's interior grace accompanies the preaching of the ministers: cf. Book One, ch. 8. Cf. below, n. 226, on the import of this conception for the supernatural character of the *gratia generalis.*

⁵¹ 1 Cor. 3. 4-9.

⁵² *Ibid.* 12. 18.

⁵³ 1 Cor. 12. 3-11.

⁵⁴ *Ibid.* 12. 11.

⁵⁵ *Ibid.* 3. 8.

⁵⁶ *Id unde,* 'the dignity'; Girard (87), 'le secours.'

⁵⁷ Matt. 25. 14 f.

⁵⁸ The passage, *Non itaque omnis reparabilis reparatus . . .,* is cited by Hincmar of Rheims (cf. n. 37 to the Intro.). The interpretation given here to the parable aims at bringing out that grace is given not for merit, but gratis. Capacity or ability for work or virtue, which is all that man has before he receives grace, does not mean work or virtue; and only from virtuous actions can merit spring. Merit, therefore, follows on grace and can never precede it. In the context where Hincmar quotes the text, he explains the three stages of man's nature in this regard: before sin man was *sanus,* after sin he is *sanabilis,* through grace he can again become *sanus.* Cf. St. Augustine, *De praed. sanct.* 6. 10: 'Posse habere fidem, sicut posse habere caritatem, naturae est hominum; habere autem fidem, quemadmodum habere caritatem, gratiae est fidelium' (see also Prosper, *Lib. sent. ex Aug. delib.* 318).

⁵⁹ *praevidebat,* 'foresaw,' or perhaps better, 'knew for himself,' 'saw before him.'

⁶⁰ Cf. Matt. 25. 21 and 23.

⁶¹ Cf. *ibid.* 25. 26 ff. Quesnel, *op. cit.* (ML 55. 354A), finds a parallel to this passage in St. Leo, *Serm,* 10; cf. Cappuyns, 'L'auteur' 221 f.

⁶² B *antequam* (read *ante quam*), M *ante quem.*

⁶³ Cf. Matt. 25. 31 ff.

⁶⁴ Compare Pelagius, *Epist. ad Demetr.* 16 (ML 30. 29 f.), 'Nec minuisse solum, sed non auxisse culpabile est.'

⁶⁵ B *ideo,* M *a Deo. Quaerantur,* 'pursue' rather than 'ask,' as Girard translates (90), 'demander.'

[66] Cf. John 12. 24.

[67] Cf. 1 Cor. 3. 7.

[68] *Habet quod ab ipso expectetur, ad id quod accepit augendum.* Cf. Girard (90), 'doit faire profiter ce qu'elle a receu, et produire le fruit qu'on attend d'elle.'

[69] Cf. above, ch. 6. The question treated in the digression is the gratuitousness of the beginning of grace in man, against the Semi-Pelagians. Grace is given to man without any merit on his part, but it is up to him to increase it. The excursus was occasioned by the idea of the inequality of the graces which are given to different men; the differences are not due to different merits antecedent to grace, since all merit comes from grace.

[70] Cf. Rom. 11. 33.

[71] Cf. Isa. 65. 1. These three periods in the history of the dispensation of graces are found in *Resp. cap. Gall.* 8.

[72] Cf. Rom. 9. 8.

[73] For these three historical stages in the economy of the salvation of men, see Book One, n. 188.

[74] Cf. Rom. 11. 33. See Book One, ch. 13.

[75] Cf. Augustine, *De corr. et grat.* 16; *De praed. sanct.* 16; *In Ioan. Ev. tract.* 53. 6.

[76] This practical attitude of mind, concluded from the much repeated principle that there are many things in the mystery of God's dispensations of grace which surpass our understanding, together with the following practical rule, that yet we must try to know what is accessible to our knowledge, characterises St. Prosper's mental outlook well, as it reveals itself in the *De vocatione*: a synthesis of a partly 'agnostic' attitude and of a practical belief in the possibility of understanding the faith. He had learned this from St. Augustine: cf. *De dono persev.* 14. 37, 'Numquid ideo negandum est quod apertum est, quia comprehendi non potest quod occultum est?' Cf. B's marginal note, 'non negligenda cognita propter incognita.'

[77] Matt. 5.45, with interchange of the clauses, as also in *Resp. cap. Vincent.* 13. In the following the term *'vitales auras'* harks back to Lucretius: *De rer. nat.* 3. 405; 5. 857; cf. also Vergil, *Aen.* 1. 387 f.

[78] Rom. 8. 14.

[79] Cf. the story of Gen. 6. 1-4. Prosper interprets the *filiae hominum* (Gen. 6. 2) as meaning the reprobate.

[80] Gen. 6. 3.

[81] Cf. Book One, chs. 2 and 6 on the spiritual will, and *ibid.* n. 37. Besides God's exterior gifts bestowed on all men, the just, or saints from the beginning of human history received interior graces—the guidance of the Holy Spirit.

[82] Ecclus. 31. 10.

[83] Prov. 8. 35 (Sept.).

[84] This idea of the gradual dispensation of God's graces is one aspect or manifestation of the inequality of God's gifts to men, and prepares the further important distinction between the *gratia generalis* and the *gratia specialis*.

[85] Cf. Heb. 7. 10.

[86] Cf. Gen. 14. 19.

[87] Cf. Rom. 4. 18.

[88] Cf. Mal. 1. 2 and Rom. 9. 13.

[89] Jer. 1. 5.

[90] Cf. Luke 1. 44.

[91] Cf. Matt. 11. 11.

[92] Mark 9. 23.

[93] Luke 17. 5.

[94] For these Augustinian ideas and views on the triad—faith, understanding, charity—cf. M. Schmaus, *Die psychologische Trinitätslehre des hl. Augustinus* (Münster i. W. 1927) 299 f. For Augustine's celebrated '*Intelligam,*' inquis, '*ut credam*': '*Crede,*' inquam, '*ut intelligas,*' see *Serm.* 43. 6. 7, and E. Gilson, *Introduction a l'étude de saint Augustin* (2nd ed. Paris 1943) 31-47.

[95] Cf. 1 John 4. 8. Cf. the same idea and the same Scripture reference in St. Augustine, *Epist.* 188 (*Ad Iulian.*) 1. 3; *Serm.* 21. 2; 156. 5. 5; Gilson, *ibid.* 183 f.

[96] Cf. Jer. 51. 7; Apoc. 14. 8 and 16.19.

[97] Cf. 1 Cor. 13. 2 f.

[98] We have here one element for the explanation of the fact that not all are saved: they who turn away from God (and they only) are forsaken by Him. Cf. *Resp. cap. Vincent.* 7, 'Deus qui priusquam deseratur, neminem deserit.' The idea comes from St. Augustine, *De nat. et grat.* 26. 29, 'non deserit si non deseratur.'

[99] Cf. below, ch. 28 and n. 270.

[100] No true virtue without grace—cf. Book One, ch. 6.

[101] Cf. Book One, ch. 2, 'Huius voluntatis, quantum ad naturalem pertinet motum *ex vitio primae praevaricationis infirmum . . . .*'

[102] The first people of God was Israel, the second will be the Christians; cf. 1 Peter 2. 9, often cited in the *De vocatione*.

[103] *praedamnati*, the reprobate. But as noted already (Intro. n. 49) and as appears from what follows, St. Prosper teaches reprobation *post praevisa merita*. The expression *praedamnati* is to be understood from the context.

[104] Gen. 4. 6 f. (Sept.).

[105] The commentary given here explains the otherwise obscure meaning of the quoted text. Cain's sin consisted in not dividing rightly between God and himself, when he reserved the better fruits of his fields for himself instead of offering these to God. His sin could have 'come back on him' through repentance and sorrow for it, and thus it was possible for him to 'take command over it.' Compare St. Augustine's reflexions on Cain's sin, in *De civ. Dei* 15. 7.

[106] B *quantum ad medendi modum*, M *quantum ad illum medendi modum*.

[107] For the reconciliation of God's foreknowledge and man's free will, cf. St. Augustine, *De civ. Dei* 5. 10. 2.

[108] . . . *multiplicatae fecunditatis tam numerosa propagatio*: cf. Gen. 4. 17-24, the generations of Cain.—Quesnel, *op. cit.* (ML 54. 165 B), found in the present passage a parallel to St. Leo's *Serm.* 10.

[109] Cf. Gen. 7. This symbolical interpretation of the story of the Flood is not uncommon with the Fathers: cf., e.g. Augustine, *De civ. Dei* 15. 26 f. See J. Daniélou, 'Déluge. Baptême, Jugement,' *Dieu Vivant* 8 (1947) 98, 112.

[110] *omnium gentium plenitudo*, the fulness of the nations which constitutes the *specialis universitas* of the elect—cf. Book One, ch. 9. Another idea implied is that of the fixed number of the elect, as conceived by St. Augustine in his doctrine on predestination; see below, ch. 29 and n. 285. Cf. Amann, *art. cit.* 1802.

[111] Cf. Gen. 9. 4; Lev. 17. 14; Acts 15. 20, 29.

[112] Cf. Gen. 9. 13 f.

[112a] . . . *mysteria atque sacramenta*.

[113] Cf. Gen. 11. 1-11.

[114] These seventy-two tongues originated at Babel according to a tradition followed, for example, by St. Augustine, *De civ. Dei* 16.4 (cf. 16. 11).

[115] Phil. 2. 11.

[116] Cf. Gen. 22. 17 and Rom. 9. 8.

[117] John 8. 56.

[118] Cf. Rom. 4. 10.

[119] John 1. 14.

[120] Gen. 22.18, 26.4, 28.14 (Acts 3.25).

[121] Cf. above, ch. 5 and nn. 46 and 47. The present text is more restrictive than the former.

[122] Eph. 2. 12.

[123] *superna doctrina*, 'teaching from heaven' or 'God's revelation,' a grace of light that is sufficient to enlighten all—*testimonium*—but leads to salvation only some. Cf. below, n. 226, the *gratia generalis*. A hint is given here as to the interior and supernatural character of this grace of light which is called *parcioris et occultioris gratiae*: the external grace is not hidden, but only an interior one.

[124] Rom. 5. 20.

[125] *plerique*, 'many.' Nothing more seems to be meant here than a poke at the Pelagian optimism believing that man, because of his free will, can be naturally good and without sin.

[126] Cf. St. Paul, Rom. 3. 9, 23, and 5. 20.

[127] Ironically, of course: they were not ready for the Gospel at all, as far as psychological preparedness was concerned.

[128] John 1. 29. B *tollentem peccata*, M *tollentem peccatum*.

[129] Ps. 2. 1 f.

[130] Acts 4. 24-28.

[131] This idea that the wicked in carrying out their evil designs are instrumental in bringing into effect the plans of God's Providence, is not original to St. Prosper: cf. St. Augustine, *De grat. et lib. arb.* 20. 41 and 21. 42; *De praed. sanct.* 16. 33.

[132] 1 John 5. 20.

[133] Col. 1. 12 f.

[134] Titus 3. 3-7.

[135] Cf. Matt. 9. 12 f.

[136] Isa. 9. 2 f.

[137] Rom. 5. 1-5.

[138] Ps. 43. 22.

[139] Rom. 8. 35-39.

[140] The Semi-Pelagians wrongly concluded from St. Augustine's teaching on predestination that Christ did not die for all men, but only for the predestined. Cf. Prosper's answer in *Resp. cap. Vincent.* 1 and *Resp. cap. Gall.* 9.

[141] Rom. 5. 6-10.

[142] 2 Cor. 5. 14 f.

[143] 1 Tim. 1. 15 f.

[144] Acts 2. 9-11.

[145] The providential preparation of the Roman Empire for the expansion of Christianity is the well-known idea of St. Leo, *Serm*. 82. 2: 'Ut autem huius inenarrabilis gratiae per totum mundum diffunderetur effectus, Romanum regnum divina providentia praeparavit.' The parallelism was naturally pointed out by Quesnel (ML 55. 353. 3). The idea itself was developed much earlier—cf. Origen, *Contra Cels*. 2. 30.

[146] *Quae tamen per apostolici sacerdotii principatum amplior facta est arce religionis, quam solio potestatis.* Cf. *Carm. de ingr.* 40-42; Leo, *Serm*. 82. 1.

[147] Girard (112) translates here a variant reading quoted by Mangeant, 'quemadmodum quasdam gentes quod ante non noverunt, in consortium filiorum Dei novimus adoptatas': 'nous sçavons qu'il se trouve quantité de peuples qui ont l'honneur d'estre désia receus au nombre des enfants de Dieu.'

[148] The stage is here set for the discussion of the problem of the salvation of infidels. Prosper admits that there may be in his own days, as there were in the past, peoples who have not heard the Gospel yet. What about them and God's salvific will?

[149] A first element of his answer: the time of their call to the Gospel is appointed by God's Providence. They will be called, though we do not know when.

[150] B *desuper*, M *de super*.

[151] A second element of the answer: the Gentiles always received the general help which God's Providence never refused to anyone. Cf. above, chs. 4 and 15.

[152] *spontanea contemplatio*, 'natural speculation'—cf. Book One, ch. 4. As has been said there already, this natural speculation cannot lead to the effective knowledge of God without *superna lux*, the divine light, called there *illuminans Dei gratia* (cf. n. 21 to Book One). If so, we have here another indication that the general help given to all is, for St. Prosper, a real grace or supernatural help.

[153] Col. 1. 26 f.

[154] B *hoc mysterium*, M *mysterium*.

[155] Deut. 32. 19-21 (Sept.).

[156] Ps. 85. 9.

[157] *Ibid*. 71. 11.

[158] *Ibid*. 71. 17.

[159] Isa. 2. 2 (Sept.).

[160] *Ibid*. 25. 6 f. (Sept.).

[161] *Ibid.* 52. 10 (Sept.).

[162] *Ibid.* 54. 15 (Sept.).

[163] *Ibid.* 55. 5 (Sept.). On the universalism of messianism in Isaias, which is the Old Testament expression of the universal salvific will, cf. A. Condamin, *Le Livre d'Isaïe* (Paris 1905) 361. Compare St. Augustine, *De civ. Dei,* 18. 29.

[164] Osee 1. 10 f. (Sept.).

[165] *Ibid.* 2. 23 f.

[166] Cf. Matt. 3. 11.

[167] Acts 11. 15-18.

[168] Amos 9. 11 f. (Sept.).

[169] Acts 15. 13-18.

[170] Luke 2. 26.

[171] *Ibid.* 2. 29-32.

[172] B begins chapter 19 here: *His et aliis testimoniis;* M cuts the sentence after *absconditum fuisse consilio,* and begins the present chapter with *Et cur hac manifestatione.*

[173] This chapter contains the explicit statement of the original contribution of the *De vocatione* to the problem of the universal salvific will: its theory of the general grace or divine help given to all men, and of a special help or grace given to the elect.

[174] *in novissimo mundi tempore,* in this last world period begun with the coming of Christ: cf. 1 Cor. 10. 11; above, Book One n. 168.

[175] Does this mean hidden—*absconditam*—in the sense of withheld, not given; or rather, when given, then done so in a hidden way? From what was said in previous chapters and what follows in the next, the idea seems rather to be that the abundance of grace was withheld in former ages, when grace was given sparingly to the non-chosen peoples.

[176] 1 Tim. 2. 4.

[177] Cf. Book One, ch. 25 and n. 358, *pars fidei.*

[178] These general gifts of grace given to all men (cf. above, ch. 15), as pointed out already (cf. nn. 123, 152) imply interior and supernatural graces. They are not restricted to the exterior grace only, to the teaching gathered from the testimony of the created world. The special gifts added to these will be explained further.

[179] Obviously the *gratia* here mentioned refers to the abundant grace of which the beginning of this chapter makes mention; cf. also above, n. 175. All men did receive the general gifts of grace which are sufficient to be for all a lesson, *omnibus in testimonium*

(cf. above, ch. 15 and n. 123); and on that account they plead guilty of malice, *de sua nequitia arguantur.* With the special gifts added to these, God's grace provides, according to the same chapter 15, a saving remedy for some, *quibusdam in remedium,* namely, for the elect who are actually saved.

¹⁸⁰ The case of the infants, of whom some happen to receive baptism and others not, has been dealt with in Book One, ch. 16, as a proof of the inscrutability of God's decrees; and in ch. 22 as an argument for the gratuitousness of the first grace. Here it is presented as an objection against the universal salvific will of which the preceding chapter proposed an explanation. The objection is this: The children who die without baptism do not seem to have received the general help of grace which was said to be given to all men.

¹⁸¹ 1 Tim. 2. 4.

¹⁸² We should recall here that for our author, as for St. Augustine, unbaptised children are condemned to hell, though theirs is *mitissima damnatio.* Cf. above, Book One n. 212.

¹⁸³ *cum peccati carne*—cf. Rom. 8. 3.

¹⁸⁴ This sentence is absent from *Vat. Reg. 293* and *Vat. Lat. 262;* 'n *Vat. Lat. 268* it is only a marginal note (Ballerini).

¹⁸⁵ Cf. Book One, nn. 273 and 274.

¹⁸⁶ B *sed quales,* M *et quales.*

¹⁸⁷ The reason for this discrimination is unknowable for us, as explained in Book One, ch. 16. Cf. Augustine, *Epist.* 194 (Ad *Sixt.*) 7. 33, '. . . cur in eadem causa super alium veniat misericordia, super alium maneat ira eius.'

¹⁸⁸ The guilt of original sin is sufficient, in our author's conception to justly condemn to hell all who die with it. Cf. above, n. 182; Augustine, *Epist.* 184A (*Ad Petr. et Abrah.*) 2: 'potest eorum merito dici in illa damnatione minima poena, non tamen nulla.'

¹⁸⁹ Regarding the hidden justice of God, cf. Book One, ch. 17 n. 219.

¹⁹⁰ The necessity of not investigating what God wants to be unknown by us, has been repeatedly stressed, e.g. Book One, ch. 13 n. 192; Book Two, ch. 1.

¹⁹¹ St. Prosper has inherited this deep awareness of the grave guilt implied in original sin from St. Augustine; cf. *De civ. Dei* 21. 12.

¹⁹² B *Nemo etiam,* M *nemo autem.*

¹⁹³ The Church officially sanctioned the doctrine that mortality,

# 206 NOTES

or the necessity to die, has originated in mankind with original sin, when she condemned Pelagius in the Sixteenth Council of Carthage. Cf. Mansi 3. 811A = Hefele-Leclercq 2. 1. 190 = ES 101.

[194] Cf. Girard (120), 'il n'est jamais tellement en possession de la vie, qu'il ne soit toujours en péril de mort.'

[195] Compare with the exposé of man's subjection to death St. Augustine, *De civ. Dei* 13. 10, 'nihil aliud tempus huius vitae quam cursus ad mortem.'

[196] Ecclus. 40. 1.

[197] The belief in the perfect justice of God's ruling in the problem of physical evil draws from the Augustinian conception of the grave malice of original sin; cf. above, n. 191.

[198] B *nihil ei,* M *nihil eis.*

[199] Justice tempered with mercy: the idea is St. Augustine's— cf., e.g. *Enarr. in Ps.* 32. 1. 10-12.

[200] An Augustinian idea flowing from his conception of the state of fallen mankind as a *massa damnationis:* cf. *De civ. Dei* 21. 12.

[201] B *decessu,* M *discessu.*

[202] Job 12. 9 f.

[203] *Ibid.* 14. 5.

[204] B *usque ad senectutem,* M *usque in senectutem.*

[205] The problem of physical evil in connection with the infants is made very acute by the assumption that unbaptised infants are condemned to hell in the next world, as St. Augustine held (cf., e.g. *Enchir.* 23. 93: ACW 3. 88) and St. Prosper after him.

[206] Here is the answer to the objection formulated in ch. 20—cf. above, n. 180. Children *did* receive a general grace.

[207] Cf. 1 Tim. 2. 4.

[208] . . . *illam gratiae partem,* that is, a 'general' grace, referred to above, ch. 19, as *dona generalia.*

[209] It is not very clear what our author means. The general grace given to the parents consists mainly in the knowledge of God drawn from things created, with the help of an interior grace of light (cf. above, Book One, ch. 4, and Book Two, ch. 4 and n. 44). This can indeed be a help for the parents who are adults, but what help does it mean for their children? Or have we to suppose that if the parents had made good use of the general grace they received, God would also have given them the special graces needed for salvation, both for themselves (the grace of the faith) and for their children (the grace of baptism)? This seems to be the implication of the whole argument. Cf. below, n. 215.

[210] *. . . sub arbitrio iacent voluntatis alienae, nec ullo modo eis nisi per alios consuli potest.*

[211] *. . . ad eorum pertinere consortium,* they are one with their parents.

[212] *Sicut enim ex aliena professione credunt:* this does not mean that the parents' profession of the faith by itself provides the faith to the children (how could it?); but that if the parents have the faith (and had, therefore, received the special graces necessary to come to the true faith), they will be instrumental in providing for their children the special grace needed for them to receive the faith, namely, baptism.

[213] *Quam ipsorum factum est nasci, tam ipsorum efficitur non renasci:* when the children are born, their existence or their having come to exist is their own concern, in the sense that they are the interested subjects of this fact and it is they who will derive the advantages implied in birth. *A pari,* the privation of baptism—*non renasci*—is also their loss or disadvantage; they have to suffer the consequences of it.—But cf. Girard (124), 'la régénération leur est aussi étrangère que la naissance leur est propre.'

[214] This application of the teaching of ch. 19 on the general and special grace, to the case of infant children, throws more light on that doctrine itself than on the problem of the children's salvation. The theory has as its background the Augustinian doctrine of election-predestination. The general grace given to all is an effect of the universal salvific will, but it is by itself insufficient for actual salvation. Only with the addition of special grace can it lead to salvation—and these special graces are given to the elect only.

[215] How does the election reveal itself in the case of children who die before the age of reason, some being baptised and others not? In general the divine election is expressed in the special graces given in addition to the general ones. The election, therefore, is revealed in the way the special graces reach the children. This is said to happen in two possible manners which are altogether different in their outcome. Either the children receive the special grace in their parents, when these have the faith; but this special grace of the parents will not in fact profit the children who die before baptism; yet the special grace, result of the election, is not withheld from them in so far as their parents have received the special grace of the faith (which is for the children—normally—the first step to the grace of baptism). Or they receive the special grace without their parents having received the same, when they

are unbelievers, and when outsiders see to the baptism of the children, thanks to a special providential disposition resulting from their election (cf. the n. following).—The first alternative may seem, and is, a purely nominal solution. These unbaptised children did not in fact receive themselves the special grace which is the effect of the election. The election therefore, though not withheld from them in so far as it has reached their parents, yet does not in fact mean anything to them personally; unless we say that it reveals itself as their non-election.

216 This care of strangers is the providential way of the election, procuring to these infants the special grace needed for actual salvation, the grace of baptism. Their own people could not do so, because they themselves were *impii*, unbelievers, and had received the general grace only. Thus the election reveals itself in this mysterious discrimination between children. Some children of believing parents fail to receive baptism; they are not among the elect. Others, children of non-Christians, happen to be baptised thanks to the care of strangers; they are objects of the divine election. Cf. *Carm. de ingr.* 632-6. St. Augustine frequently pointed to these same facts (some children of baptised parents die without baptism; others of unbelieving parents die after baptism) to bring out his views on predestination: note *Epist.* 194. (*Ad Sixt.*) 7. 32; *De grat. et lib. arb.* 23. 45; *De corr. et grat.* 8. 18.

217 The chapter answers the unformulated objection: But why does not God provide the special grace of actual baptism for all children? Is not that unjust?

218 The answer is: God would give the special grace of baptism to all children if this were necessary because of His justice or mercy. But as will be proved instantly, it is not necessary.

219 B *quantum in cordibus,* M *quantum cordibus.*

220 A first proof that it is not necessary for God always to provide baptism for all children, but rather better not to provide it: if He did, the certainty of baptism would cause the faithful to be negligent about having their children receive it.

221 According to this second argument, the Pelagians could say that children are not excluded from heaven, not because Providence always sees to their baptism, but because they are without sin and thus have a claim to happiness.

222 *Habet gratia quod adoptet, non habet unda quod diluat*—a Pelagian formula found in the anonymous work *Hypomnesticon* (or *Hypognosticon*) *contra Pelagianos et Caelestianos* 5. 8. 13 (ML

45. 1656). On this ps.-Augustinian work, variously ascribed to Marius Mercatur and Pope Sixtus III, cf. Bardenhewer, *op. cit.* 4. 479.—A marginal note in B reads, 'dogma Pelagianum.'

[223] See the reference to the condemnation in the Sixteenth Council of Carthage of the Pelagian doctrine on the baptism of children—above, Book One, ch. 22 and n. 274.

[224] The conclusion of this chapter once more reveals our author's keen sense of original sin, which is at the root of this acceptance of God's just judgment on the unbaptised children. Today an additional element for an answer is drawn from the doctrine on Limbo which was unknown in St. Prosper's time (see above, n. 212 to Book One).

[225] In this chapter we have a precise statement of Prosper's conception of the universal salvific will: God wills all men to be saved without exception—meaning that He gives grace to all, though not to all in the same degree. All receive a general grace, and only some a special grace; and these alone actually attain salvation.

[226] Cf. above, chs. 4 and 19.—Is this general grace only an exterior help or is it also interior? From the present passage it would seem to be merely exterior; at any rate, only the exterior help is mentioned explicitly. Yet, as the Ballerini brothers already noted, *Observationes in Dissert. II Quesnelli* 17 (ML 55. 380D), and recently Cappuyns, 'L'auteur' 204 n. 2, the *gratia generalis* of the *De vocatione* comprises both exterior and interior divine help. At times the interior help is stated explicitly (1. 4; 2. 4, 17. 25), in other places only the exterior testimony of things created is mentioned (1. 5; 2. 25). Even then in St. Prosper's conception an interior help is indirectly postulated. For, according to a frequently expressed view of his, all grace, either special or general, if it is to lead to any good results, requires both exterior and interior help. The special grace, as found in the Law and Prophets or in the Gospel, remains ineffective without interior grace (2. 7); so also the general grace which is the testimony of created things (2. 4). Whenever the general grace was effective, this was due to an interior grace (2. 5), just as for the Law (1. 8) and the Gospel (*ibid.*). Another confirmation of this lies in the statement often repeated that the difference between special and general grace is one of degree only—of greater abundance or scarcity (2. 19, 23, 25), not of kind. It is always the grace of the Redeemer, Christ (2. 5, 9, 15). St. Prosper's opposition to the Pelagian conception

of an exterior grace (1. 8) makes it altogether improbable that he would call grace a merely exterior help.

Should it not be said that the interior help added to the exterior teaching or preaching of the created things is the special grace, so that exterior grace is the same as general, and interior the same as special grace? This does not seem to be the idea of the *De vocatione*. Both the Law and the Prophets, and the Gospel, which are exterior graces, are called *gratia specialis* (2. 4, 9), and at the same time it is said explicitly that they cannot actually lead to salvation without an interior action of God in the soul (1. 8; 2. 4). If general grace meant exterior help only, then no one could ever profit by it. If special grace meant only interior help, then there would be no reason why Israel or the Christians would be considered as privileged; for then what they have received more in the line of exterior help, the Law or the Gospel, would always remain a grace that can lead nowhere without the addition of an interior grace. But it is said explicitly that the call to the Gospel is a special one (2. 23), just as was the direction provided by the Law for Israel (2. 9). Both the special grace, therefore, and the general one comprise exterior and interior help from God.

²²⁷ We already know St. Prosper's insistence on the unknowability of the reasons or motives of God's decrees and judgments about the dispensation of grace; cf. below, n. 290.

²²⁸ If all men received the same graces, the question would no longer arise why this man receives one grace and that one another. There would be no question of mysterious reasons for a diversity. This was exactly Pelagius' position: 'Nam cum universa turba credentium paria dona gratiae percipiat et iisdem omnes sacramentorum benedictionibus glorientur . . .' (Cf. de Plinval, *Pélage* 230).

²²⁹ Then His special grace would no longer appear as something special and surprising, since it would be the same for all.

²³⁰ How does this follow? God's general kindness would remain a grace, since all would be able to know their Maker from His gifts; but there would be no special grace any more: no particular gifts, given to some and not given to others, would strikingly bring out the gratuitousness of all God's gifts.

²³¹ The meaning seems to be that God did not refuse to all mankind the special grace, since He gives it to some of them. Perhaps this implies that God was *ready* to give the special grace to all, but that some refused to accept it; the proof of His readiness to give

more being precisely the general grace which He actually gives to all. Cf. the following n.

[232] This apparently insinuates that the reason why special graces are not given to all is because in some men 'nature recoiled,' that is, because they did not want to accept them. But would this be consistent with the election theory of our author? Hardly. At any rate, he does not explain it further. If we understand these lines in this sense, that they lay the reason why God withholds His special graces from some in the free will of men who refuse to accept them, then his solution of the universal salvific will becomes considerably more satisfactory. For then it comes to mean that the special grace needed for actual salvation is offered to all, but not actually given to some because they refuse it. This, however, is inconsistent with our author's views on the election (cf. above, ch. 23) according to which God reveals His mercy in some men through special graces, and in others, His justice. But cf. Intro. n. 56. Cf. *Resp. cap. Vincent.* 7, 'Quamdiu salvi esse nolunt, salvi esse non possunt.'

[233] The problem examined in the present chapter is not how to reconcile grace and free will, but only to show the fact that free will remains as a necessary but secondary factor in the process of justification. We are reminded of St. Augustine in the *De grat. et lib. arb.*, but perhaps there is more insistence on the active co-operation of man's will. Are we to see here an indication that the *resiluisse naturam* of the previous chapter (n. 232) is to be taken as a refusal of grace?

[234] Grace would do violence to the human will if God's will did everything in a man's salvation without the free co-operation of man. This would be against the free nature of man's will. But the will is associated with grace.

[235] Even in the case of the justification of children God does not do alone the whole work since another man's will intervenes. They who bring the children to baptism co-operate with God.

[236] As was explained above, n. 232, and is explicitly stated here, both exterior and interior aids belong to the *gratia specialis.*

[237] The co-operation of free will and grace, expressed here, comes to this: grace has the initiative in stirring the will and enabling it to act; thus moved and enabled, the will co-operates with the gift given in order to gain merit.

[238] It is worth pointing out that St. Prosper explicitly attributes the virtuous actions done with the help of grace to both grace *and*

free will. In this point he differs from St. Augustine who stresses the role of grace to the extent of obscuring the part of the free will.—Girard (161) reads here the distinction between sufficient grace (given to all) and efficacious grace (made thus through free co-operation).

[239] The positive counterpart of this negative statement, namely, that virtue is given to all who wish to be virtuous (and there is no true virtue without grace), is found nowhere in the *De vocatione*. We may not, therefore, deduce from this negative sentence that a lack of good will is the only reason why virtue is not given. This would run counter to the election doctrine, according to which God gives or does not give His graces as He pleases, for reasons of His own which we cannot know.

[240] When grace is said to act through teaching or through fear, we must remember that in our author's conception exterior grace is not isolated but doubled with interior grace; cf. above, n. 226.

[241] Prov. 9. 10.

[242] Ecclus. 25. 15.

[243] *Quae auctore gratiae eodem proficit timore quo coepit*: both B and M follow this reading, and note the variant, '*quo* auctore.' The meaning is much the same: the fear of the Lord is the source of progress as it was the beginning of virtue. Cf. Girard (129), 'qui est cause du progrès, non moins que du commencement de la grâce.'

[244] Cf. Book One, ch. 8, on the healing effects of grace.

[245] Cf. Book One, ch. 6—no true virtue without grace.

[246] . . . *nisi oculos in eo aperuerit voluntatis*: the eyes of the will, that is, the eyes of the soul that should direct the will. It should be noted that Prosper frequently calls grace a light, implying in this more than mere knowledge—a desire and inclination to act accordingly. Cf. Book One, ch. 8, on the interior action of grace which goes together with the exterior grace. In this also we find an Augustinian idea: that grace is superior to the Law in that it not only shows what is to be done, but gives the desire and the strength to do what is commanded: cf. *De spir. et litt.* 19. 32.

[247] Cf. ch. 11.

[248] John 6. 44.

[249] Matt. 16. 17.

[250] Cf. above, ch. 26.

[251] Cf. St. Augustine, *Conf.* 13. 9. 10, 'Pondus meum amor meus; eo feror, quocumque feror.'

[252] *Et quod eos voluit Deus velle, voluerunt*: cf. St. Agustine, *Contra duas epist. Pelag.* 1. 19. 37, '. . . ut volentes ex nolentibus fiant'; *Epist.* 186 (*Ad Paulin.*) 2. 6, 'Recolat utrum quaesierit, an quaesitus sit.'

[253] Repeated stress on the fact that free will remains under the action of grace, that the election does not put aside freedom. Girard (164 f.) comments: efficacious grace and free will.

[254] Matt. 26. 41. Cf. the same argumentation on this text in St. Augustine, *De grat. et lib. arb.* 4. 9.

[255] Luke 22. 31 f.

[256] *Ibid.* 22. 40.

[257] B *pro eo,* M *pro ea.*

[258] B *negationem eius,* M *negationem Christi.*

[259] . . . *conturbatum cor Apostoli non humanis sed divinis convenit oculis;* cf. St. Leo, *Serm.* 54. 5, 'illis turbatum discipulum convenit oculis'—a parallel among several which Quesnel pointed out, *op. cit.* (ML 55. 353 BC).

[260] John 10. 18.

[261] Gal. 5. 17.

[262] Matt. 26. 41.

[263] Cf. Job 7. 1.

[264] Cf. above, Book One, ch. 8 and n. 81, on the usefulness of struggle and temptation.

[265] John 21. 18 f.

[266] . . . *quae ab illa principali petra communionem et virtutis sumpsit et nominis*: cf. Leo, *Epist.* 28. 5, '. . . a principali petra soliditatem et virtutis traxit et nominis'; cf. Quesnel, *op. cit.* (ML 55. 353C).

[267] Matt. 6. 13.

[268] 1 Cor. 1. 31.

[269] B *victoriam,* M *gloriam.*

[270] Cf. above, ch. 12. A similar idea is found in Pelagius' *Epist. ad Demetr.* 3: 'Nec esset omnino virtus ulla in bono perseverantis, si is ad malum transire non potuisset' (ML 30. 17D).

[271] Note once more the stress on freedom which remains under the action of grace and with the gift of perseverance.

[272] 1 Tim. 2. 4.

[273] The present chapter is perhaps the most striking example of Prosper's struggle to synthesize the Augustinian doctrine on elec-

tion-predestination with his own universalistic conception of the divine salvific will; perhaps it is also another proof of his inconsistency in holding on to both doctrines which, when taken rigidly, are irreconcilable.

274 Isa. 40. 8.

275 *praescita et promissa*: the term *praedestinata* is avoided; *gentium plenitudo*: a restricted totality—cf. Book One, ch. 9 and nn. 127, 137.

276 Cf. Book One, ch. 9, where the promise is interpreted in a restrictive sense.

277 Cf. John 6. 39.

278 Cf. *ibid.* 10. 29.

279 2 Tim. 2. 19.

280 *Quod et nemini negatur et nemini debetur, in its quos promisit, efficitur*—the grace which is given to the men that are comprised in the promise(= election = predestination) is refused to no one. How to understand this? Is the *specialis gratia* without which there is no salvation, and with which there is, offered to all men? Is it not actually given to all only because they refuse to accept it? Cf. above, n. 232, and below, n. 284. If so, this can hardly be reconciled with the election-predestination doctrine.

281 1 Cor. 12. 6.

282 *iusta et bona*: God's justice and goodness or mercy are manifested in the distribution of His gifts, tempering each other. Cf. above, ch. 22 and n. 199.

283 Ps. 24. 10.

284 The special graces which up to now were apparently said to be given only to the elect (cf. ch. 25), are said here to have been given also to some men who stray from the path of truth and life. This is also implied further in this chapter, *nullo excidente de plenitudine promissionum, qui . . . nec auxilio defuturus*. Must we think of a double kind of *gratia specialis*, one given to the elect only, another given also to some who will not persevere? Cf. below, ch. 33 and n. 305.

285 In God's foreknowledge the number of the elect is fixed: an Augustinian idea; cf. Augustine, *De corr. et grat.* 23. 39, 'Certum vero esse numerum electorum, neque augendum, neque minuendum.'

286 By granting to all the *gratia generalis*—cf. above, ch. 25.

287 Their malice consisted in not making use of the general gifts of grace given to all men, or even—according to what was said here

(cf. n. 284)—in misusing or leaving unused the special graces given to some who do not persevere.

288 Cf. 1 Tim. 2. 4.

289 Gal. 5. 6.—Cf. Book One, chs. 23 and 24.

290 The frequent reference (in not less than 10 chs. in Book One, and 12 in Book Two) to the mysterious and hidden things in the economy of divine grace which are beyond all human knowledge, besides passing allusions to the same mystery, is one more Augustinian feature of the *De vocatione*. Cf. St. Augustine, e.g. *De pecc. mer.* 1. 21. 29; 2. 18.32; *De spir. et litt.* 35. 61; 36. 66; *Epist.* 194 (*Ad Sixt.*) 3. 10; and the classical citation from St. Paul, Rom. 11. 33, *O altitudo.* . . . If we summarize St. Prosper's ideas in this connection, we come to the following. God has reserved to Himself certain truths which are beyond human investigation (1. 20, 21). He has not revealed them to us because it was unnecessary for us to know them. Had it been necessary, He would have made them known (1. 13, 14). These truths, therefore, we need not try to find out, we must stop at the limit of our human knowledge (1. 1, 15; 2. 1, 10, 21). And what are these unknowable truths? They are mainly the reasons or motives of God's ways in the economy of His grace and the election (1. 13, 14, 18, 21; 2. 25, 30): why He saves some and not others (2. 1); why He bestows such gifts on one and others on another (1. 17); why He acts with regard to the salvation of men, in different ways at different times (1. 13; 2. 9) and for different persons and nations (1. 15; 2. 22). We know the differences, we cannot know the reasons (2. 22). The answer to the *why* of all these differences lies with the inscrutable decrees and judgments of God which are mysterious and hidden, but cannot but be just (2. 1, 3, etc.).

291 Each item of this enumeration has been dealt with in previous chapters: different times, cf. the three periods in the history of the salvation of mankind—Book One, n. 188; different nations, that is, especially Israel and the Gentiles—cf. Book One, ch. 21; different families, cf. above, ch. 3; the infants, Book One, ch. 16; the unborn have not been mentioned explicitly in the *De vocatione* (but St. Augustine mentions them, for the case of Esau and Jacob—*Epist.* 194 [*Ad Sixt.*] 8. 35 and *Epist.* 286 [*Ad Paulin.*] 4. 14 f.); twins, see the allusion to the classical proof for the gratuitousness of grace derived from Esau and Jacob—above, ch. 11 and n. 88; also *Carm. de ingr.* 637-47; St. Augustine, *Contra duas epist. Pelag.* 2. 7. 15.

²⁹² Rom. 8. 24.

²⁹³ 1 Cor. 2. 9.

²⁹⁴ Compare this expression of the author's modesty with Book One, ch. 1.

²⁹⁵ 1 Tim. 4. 10.

²⁹⁶ Another reading noted by M has *subtilissimae veritatis* instead of *brevitatis*. B does not mention it.

²⁹⁷ These special helps are the *gratia specialis* of the elect. The special grace given to some who will not persevere (cf. above, n. 284) is not meant here.

²⁹⁸ Book Two, ch. 6.

²⁹⁹ The illustrations are aimed at Pelagius' objection against the inequality of graces, namely, that God is *acceptor personarum*. Cf. above, n. 224 to Book One. St. Augustine had answered the objection, e.g. *Contra duas epist. Pelag.* 2. 7. 13.

³⁰⁰ Cf. above, ch. 8; also Book One, ch. 24.

³⁰¹ The present chapter holds on, except for the word itself, to St. Augustine's predestination doctrine. It would seem to weaken to some degree what has been explained in the previous chs. 19 and 25 on the universal call of all men through general graces.

³⁰² The previous chapter treated of these.

³⁰³ . . . *qui perire non debeat,* who is not a reprobate: cf. Intro. n. 49, for Prosper's conception of reprobation.

³⁰⁴ Contrast with this the non-universal promulgation of the Gospel as expressed above, ch. 17; see also *Resp. cap. Gall.* 4 and *Carm. de ingr.* 275 f.

³⁰⁵ *specialis vocatio,* the special call expressed in the Gospel, has become universal. Perhaps this special call is not the same as the special grace, or it is only the special grace given also to those who will not persevere. It is, moreover, only as such an exterior grace. Cf. above, nn. 226 and 284.

³⁰⁶ This is commonly pointed out as an indication that the *De vocatione* was written in Rome.

³⁰⁷ This Christian view of Providence making all events contribute to carry out its designs is, as is well-known, the fundamental idea of St. Augustine's philosophy of history and of his *De civitate Dei.* Cf. C. Dawson, 'The City of God,' in *A Monument to Saint Augustine* (London 1930) 43 ff.

³⁰⁸ B *provectuum,* M *proventuum.*

³⁰⁹ This apparently paradoxical expression of God's eternal prescience is a reminiscence from St. Augustine, *De civ. Dei* 22. 2:

'Secundum illam vero voluntatem suam, quae cum eius praescientia sempiterna est, . . . etiam futura iam fecit.' Girard here translates (143), 'et il a désia déterminé les récompenses après avoir conclu les mérites.'

[310] Eph. 1. 3-6.—B *per Iesum Christum in ipso,* M omits *in ipso.* The present Scripture quotation is the only place in the *De vocatione* where we find the word *praedestinare.*

[311] Negative reprobation, or non-inclusion in the number of the elect.

[312] Again predestination without the name. Cf. below, n. 316.

[313] Compare the Augustinian idea of the *numerus clausus* of the elect (above, n. 285). Both aspects of it, *neque augendus neque minuendus,* are developed in this chapter.

[314] 2 Tim. 1. 8 f.

[315] These were the difficulties of the Hadrumetan monks against St. Augustine's teaching on predestination. See Augustine's *De gratia et libero arbitrio* and *De correptione et gratia.*

[316] St. Prosper's answer to the difficulties considers only God's foreknowledge, while the election-predestination implies also the part of God's will or God's choice. It may be helpful to synthetise here the dispersed elements of our author's election theory. This conception states that the sons of the promise, foreknown and foreordained (1. 9, 20) before all times (2. 33), are all saved without exception (1. 9; 2. 29), chosen as they are without any merit of their own (1. 22, 25) for reasons that remain hidden in God's omnipotent will (1. 16, 18, 20). Thus, in the sight of God mankind is divided into two sections (1. 10), one of the elect and the other of of the reprobate (2. 33). The number of the elect is fixed (2. 29, 33), God's eternal foreknowledge of it cannot fail (*ibid.*). The elect are infallibly, though freely, led to salvation, with special graces in addition to the general graces given to all (2. 25, 28), out of mere mercy (1. 25; 2. 29); while the non-elect receive in the end the just punishment of their sin (1. 25; 2. 29). The non-elect did not receive the special graces of the elect, but only the general graces, or at most the special graces that do not grant perseverance (2. 29). Even the children are condemned justly on account of original sin (2. 21). No one is lost except the reprobate (2. 33).

Why were the special graces not given to the reprobate? A twofold answer is given: the one, more stressed and more explicit, is that we do not know the reasons for God's unequal distribution of graces (1. 13, 15; 2. 9, 22, 24); the other, stated more in passing and only insinuated, is that nature recoiled (2. 25), or men refused them (2.28 *fin.*), since God abandons no one unless man first turns away from Him. (2. 12).

Is this different from St. Augustine's doctrine on predestination? His classical definition of it reads (*De dono persev.* 14. 35): 'Est praedestinatio sanctorum . . . praescientia . . . et praeparatio beneficiorum Dei, quibus certissime liberantur quicumque liberantur.' In St. Prosper's theory of election there is one element of difference: election is mainly considered as God's infallible prescience. Yet the other aspect, regarding the will, is not excluded, as appears from the much used terms, *praescitum et praeordinatum* (1. 9), *praecogniti et praeordinati* (1. 20), *praecognita et praeelecta* (2. 33). The main identity between predestination and election is the necessity of salvation for the elect and the certainty of non-salvation for the reprobate.

³¹⁷ This was the Semi-Pelagian objection against predestination; cf. *Resp. cap. Gall.* 11.

³¹⁸ St. Augustine's teaching on the negative nature of evil is well-known; cf., e.g. *Opus imp. c. Iul.* 3. 206, 'Nulla enim natura, in quantum natura est, malum est.'

³¹⁹ B *propriis*, M *proprio*.

³²⁰ This chapter answers the first objection formulated in the previous one against the election, that it would render good works unnecessary.

³²¹ 1 John 3. 8.

³²² Rom. 5. 3-5.

³²³ Eph. 2. 8-10.

³²⁴ Cf. above, ch. 8.

³²⁵ B and M correct the text to read *cum etiam ad hoc ut operentur electi sint;* while Girard translates (148) the uncorrected text quoted by Mangeant—*ad hoc operentur ut electi sint*—with 'veu mesme qu'ils travaillent pour estre elus.'

³²⁶ Matt. 25. 29.

³²⁷ Cf. Ps. 1. 2.

³²⁸ Cf. 2 Tim. 3. 12.

³²⁹ The chapter gives the answer to the second objection against election: it would make prayer superfluous.

³³⁰ B *accipere debere uxorem*, M *accipere uxorem*.

³³¹ Tob. 6. 16-18 (Sept.).

³³² This reason why God's decrees about the election must remain hidden from our knowledge, namely, in order that we may

continue in good works and prayer, was not given before in the *De vocatione*. Cf. St. Augustine, *De corr. et grat.* 13. 40: 'Nam propter huius utilitatem secreti, ne forte quis extollatur, sed omnes, etiam qui bene currunt, timeant, dum occultum est qui perveniant . . .'; *De dono persev.* 13. 33.

[333] 1 Cor. 10. 12.

[334] Ps. 144. 14.

[335] Cf. St. Augustine, *De corr. et grat.* 15. 46; also the parallel in St. Leo, *Serm.* 34. 5, 'nullius desperanda salus' (cf. Quesnel, *op. cit.*, ML 55. 353D).

[336] See above, Book One, ch. 12 and n. 178.

[337] 1 Tim. 2. 4.

# INDEX

# INDEX

Abel, 110

Abraham, father of all the nations, 67; faith of, 67, 113; God's promise to, 113, fufilled every day, 44, 67; sons of, 42, 44, 67, 91, 103

Adam, 33; sin of, 63, 127

adoption, as sons of God, 44, 146, 147; of grace, 132, 146; preceded all times, 147

adults, justified gratuitously, 70, 71, 191

adulterous woman, 38, 178

Alès, A. d', 165, 166, 169

Altaner, B., 163

Amann, E., 158-60, 163, 164, 165, 168, 171, 184, 201

Ambrose, St., 7 f., 161, 169

agnostic attitude, 185, 199

angels, 103

animal will, see will; desires, 28

Antelmi, J., 7, 161

anthropomorphism, 185

anti-Augustinism, 4 f.

Arand, L. A., 172, 181

ark of Noe, symbolism of, 111 f., 201

arts, useful, 29

astrology, 56, 186

Augustine, St., 3; and Semi-Pelagians, 3 f.; relations with St. Prosper, 4 f.; and salvific will, 11, 171. See election, predestination

   *Conf.* 13. 9. 10: 213; *C. duas ep. Pel.* 1. 19. 37: 213; 2. 5. 9: 189, 191; 2. 6. 11: 191; 2. 7. 13: 215; 2. 7. 14: 187; 2. 7. 15:

215; 4. 6. 16: 185; *C. Iul. Pelag.* 4. 3. 17: 175; 4. 3. 22: 173; *De civ. Dei:* 216; 5. 1-7: 186; 5. 8: 186; 5. 10. 2: 201; 5. 15: 173; 11. 2: 174; 12. 27. 2: 187; 13. 2: 172; 13. 10: 206; 15. 6: 178; 15. 7: 201; 15. 26 f.: 201; 16. 4: 201; 16. 11: 201; 18. 29: 204; 18. 47: 197; 19. 25: 175; 21. 12: 188, 205, 206; 22. 2. 2: 216; *De corr. et grat.:* 4, 217; 7. 13: 172; 7. 13 f.: 180; 7. 16: 180; 8. 17: 171; 8. 18: 157; 9. 20: 180; 12. 36: 180; 13. 39: 214; 13. 40: 219; 14. 44: 181; 15. 46: 219; 15. 47: 165, 184; 16: 199; *De div. quaest.* 83. 40: 186; 44: 175; *De dono persev.:* 5, 193; 7. 17: 188; 8. 17 f.: 195; 9. 21 f.: 180, 187; 11. 27: 186; 13. 33: 166, 219; 14. 35: 218; 14. 37: 199; 18. 47: 183; 20. 53: 193; *De Gen. ad litt.* 10. 17. 30: 186; *De gest. Pel.* 14. 33: 190; *De grat. Christi* 1. 7-14: 178; 1. 22. 23: 189; *De grat. et lib. arb.:* 4, 211, 217; 4. 9: 213; 15. 31: 176; 20. 41: 202; 21. 42: 202; 21. 43: 188; 22. 44: 185, 187; 23. 45: 208; *De nat. et grat.* 26. 29: 200; *De pecc. mer.* 1. 21. 29: 215; 2. 17. 26: 177; 2. 18. 32: 215; *De perf. iust. hom.* 2. 4: 177; *De praed. sanct.:* 5, 193; 1. 2: 179; 2. 3: 159; 6. 10: 198; 8. 14: 165; 8. 16: 186; 12. 23: 191; 12. 24:

# ANCIENT CHRISTIAN WRITERS

## The Works of the Fathers in Translation

*Edited by*

J. QUASTEN, S. T. D., and J. C. PLUMPE, Ph. D.